Elizabeth Gaskell

North and South

Adaptation and activities by
Jane Elizabeth Cammack
Illustrated by **Chiara Fedele**

Listen to the audio on your smartphone

1 Download the **DeALink** App

2 Use the App to scan the page

3 Listen to the audio

Content editor: Maria Grazia Donati
Design: Sara Fabbri, Erika Barabino
Page layout: Annalisa Possenti
Picture research: Alice Graziotin

Art Director: Nadia Maestri

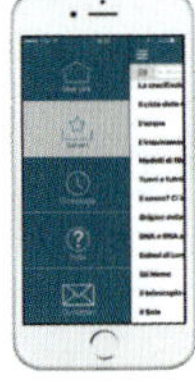

The design, production and distribution of educational materials for the CIDEB brand are managed in compliance with the rules of Quality Management System which fulfils the requirements of the standard ISO 9001 (Rina Cert. No. 24298/02/S - IQNet Reg. No. IT-80096)

Picture credits:
Shutterstock; iStockphoto; Private Collection/Bridgeman Images:4; Paul Fearn/Alamy Stock Photo: 5; lee avison/ Alamy Stock Photo: 6; SSPL/Getty Images: 78; Photo © Brian Seed/Bridgeman Images: 81; BBC/WebPhoto: 82, 83; Historica Graphica Collection/Heritage Images/Getty Images: 84; Victoria & Albert Museum, London, UK/ Bridgeman Images: 85; lowefoto / Alamy Stock Photo: 114.

Printed in Italy, by Litoprint s.r.l., Genoa

We would be happy to give you further information concerning our material and receive your comments.

info@blackcat-cideb.com
blackcat-cideb.com

Contents

Elizabeth Gaskell

Elizabeth Cleghorn Stevenson was born in Chelsea, London, in 1810. Her mother died when she was just over a year old, so she was sent to live with her mother's sister Aunt Hannah Lumb. Her brother John, who was in the merchant navy, encouraged her to write and it seems from Elizabeth's letters that she was already writing stories when she left school. However, no early stories have survived.

When Elizabeth met William Gaskell in 1831 they shared a love of music and literature, but in spite of this they were very different. Elizabeth was a lively, beautiful and sociable woman while William had a dry sense of humour and often liked to be alone. The Gaskell family lived in Manchester and had four daughters. When a young son died, William encouraged Elizabeth to write a novel. Elizabeth could see the social tensions in the city of Manchester. It had grown rapidly and was a wealthy city, but there was a lot of poverty. Her first novel, *Mary Barton*, published anonymously in 1848, was about the terrible lives of the poor workers in the industrial cities of the north.

This novel attracted the attention of Charles Dickens and much of her subsequent work was published in the periodicals which were edited by Dickens: *All the Year Round* and *Household Words*. Dickens said she had a natural talent for storytelling. Her interest in people from all classes, whether mill workers or owners, shopkeepers or doctors, brought a richness to her writing. Her very popular novel, *Cranford*, a story of two sisters and their circle of women friends, appeared in episodes from September 1851 to May 1853. It is a story that is full of humour.

Elizabeth's second Manchester novel, *North and South*, appeared in twenty-two weekly instalments in *Household Words* from September 1854 to January 1855. In June 1855 it was published in book form. Elizabeth refused to allow Dickens to edit *North and South*.

Elizabeth Gaskell had a busy social life and was a friend of Florence Nightingale before she left to nurse soldiers in the Crimean War. Elizabeth was a contemporary of William Makepeace Thackeray, George Eliot and the Brontë sisters. She was a friend of Charlotte Brontë and wrote *The Life of Charlotte Brontë* in 1857. Because of complaints about this book and legal threats, she published a revised edition.

▶ Elizabeth Gaskell's home in Manchester.

Elizabeth Gaskell was an independent spirit and travelled a lot with her children in Britain and Europe. She died suddenly in 1865 at her new home in Hampshire. She had bought the house as a surprise for her husband and family.

1 Comprehension check • **Decide if these sentences are true (T) or false (F). Correct the false statements.**

1. Elizabeth was brought up by her mother.   **T F**
2. She wrote while at school, despite no early stories surviving.   **T F**
3. Both Elizabeth and her husband were not very sociable.   **T F**
4. Elizabeth failed to notice the social tensions in Manchester.   **T F**
5. She published her first novel, *Mary Barton*, anonymously.   **T F**
6. Subsequent work was published in Dickens's magazines.   **T F**
7. Elizabeth only wrote about the working classes.   **T F**
8. Dickens didn't edit *North and South*.   **T F**
9. Elizabeth never met Florence Nightingale.   **T F**
10. People were not happy about the book she wrote on Charlotte
    Brontë.   **T F**

From top to bottom, left to right:
Margaret Hale, John Thorton, Mrs Thorton, Bessie, Nicholas Higgins,
Mr Hale, Mrs Hale, Frederick, Dixon, Edith, Henry Lennox.

1 **Match the words to the pictures.**

> maid   gentleman   Corfu   railway   puff of smoke   vicar
> cotton   cottage   shilling   pear   platform   wallpaper

2 **Use a dictionary to find the meaning of the words and choose the odd one out for each category, as in the example.**

0. job: worker   unemployed   employee   labourer

1. money: surplus   income   loss   profit

2. conflict: order   strike   riot   dispute

3. produce: make   manufacture   study   assemble

4. materials: food   wool   cotton   textile

5. income: earnings   wage   salary   debt

6. buildings: office   mill   house   factory

7. manager: worker   owner   boss   landlord

8. rights: workers' organisation   workers' group   Union   management

9. well-being: energy   disease   health   fitness

3 **Use some of the words from the exercise 2 to complete the text on cotton mills.**

In *North and South*, Milton is really the city of Manchester and Darkshire is a county that doesn't exist. The name Darkshire represents a smoky, industrial county.

During the Industrial Revolution, Manchester was the most important city for the **(1)** m.................... of **(2)** t.................... . People called it 'Cottonopolis' because by 1813 there were eighty-six cotton **(3)** m.................... . A cotton mill was a **(4)** f.................... where cotton was made into thread. Mill **(5)** o.................... imported cotton because it was cheap to buy. Cotton became more important for business than **(6)** w.................... and made large **(7)** p.................... for the mill owners. The mill **(8)** w.................... lived in small houses nearby because **(9)** w.................... were not good, but the money was better than agricultural work. People worked long hours to keep the machines going. The work was repetitive and there were accidents.

It was normal, in the 19th century, for children from poor families to work and give their **(10)** e.................... to the family. Some started work when they were four or five years old.

The conditions in the mills were not good for people's **(11)** h.................... . The air was full of dust and caused chest and lung **(12)** d.................... . Many factory owners asked their workers to sign 'The Document.' This was a promise that they would not join a **(13)** U.................... and would not **(14)** s.................... . The workers did not have any **(15)** r.................... .

A marriage and a proposal

'Edith.'

Margaret spoke gently to her cousin, but she had 

fallen asleep on the sofa. How beautiful she looked, thought Margaret. They had grown up together, but it was only now, when Edith was about to be married, that Margaret found herself considering Edith's qualities. Edith was an only child and, even though she was a little spoilt, she was very sweet.

Life was going to change for both of them. Edith and Captain Lennox were getting married and they were moving to Corfu with the regiment.[1] Margaret Hale, who was nineteen, a year older than Edith, was going to live with her parents again in the beautiful southern village of Helstone.

---

1. **regiment :** a unit of the army.

Margaret was excited about going home, but it would be strange to leave London. She had lived with Aunt Shaw for almost ten years in a beautiful house in Harley Street. Margaret's father was a poor vicar and her parents had sent her to London to enjoy life in the city.

Margaret thought that her mother and aunt were jealous of each other. Despite the fact that Aunt Shaw had not married for love, Mrs Hale was jealous of her sister's wealth. Although her marriage to General Shaw had been based on respect, she did not want that for her only child. Captain Lennox was tall and handsome and Edith loved him, of course. It was just unfortunate that the Captain did not have a beautiful house or a title.

Neighbours came to the house for dinner that evening and a little later the Captain's brother arrived. He was a lawyer called Henry Lennox and although Margaret liked him and considered him a friend, she was not in love with him. When he sat next to her, she knew she would have a pleasant evening.

'Tell me about Helstone,' he said to Margaret. 'Is it a village or a town?'

'Oh, it's too small to be called a village. There's a church and a few cottages near the green and roses round the doorways.'

'Your description is like a picture,' said Henry. 'I would like to visit you at Helstone.'

'I hope you will,' said Margaret. 'Then you will see what a beautiful place it is.'

Margaret watched him for the rest of the evening. He was intelligent but not handsome. She didn't like the sarcastic[2] way he observed everything.

Because there had not been enough money for Margaret's mother to buy a new dress and bonnet, she didn't come to Edith's wedding

---

2. sarcastic : sharp humour.

and stayed at home. Margaret returned to Helstone in late July. She loved being outside more than inside the house. She loved the forest and the people who worked on the land. Margaret hated business or anything to do with industry.

In the years Margaret had been away, her mother had grown discontented with her life. She wanted her husband to take on a bigger parish[3] with more money and responsibility. Mr Hale also seemed troubled and spent every evening in his study reading. Margaret thought they were hiding some bad news about her brother Frederick who was still away at sea. They had heard from him, but there was something they were not telling her.

One beautiful day Mr Henry Lennox visited them. It was one of Mrs Hale's days when everything was difficult.

'But we will have to give Mr Lennox dinner and there is nothing but cold meat. And your father is depressed.'

When Margaret's mother spoke, it was like a cold cloud coming between her and the sun. 'Cold meat is fine. I'm going to take Mr Lennox outside. We can do some drawing.'

And everything was fine until Henry drew a picture of Margaret speaking to one of the old men who lived in the cottages. She wasn't sure why, but it made her feel uncomfortable. After dinner they walked in the garden together.

Suddenly he took her hand. 'Margaret, I hope you have missed London and your friends there. I don't want you to like Helstone so much. I don't have much to offer you at the moment, but I love you.'

Margaret tried to calm herself. 'I didn't know you felt like this, Henry. You are a friend. I would like us to continue to be friends.'

'At least give me hope that one day our friendship can turn to love?'

---

3. parish : a church and community.

'I can't, Henry. Let's forget this conversation ever happened.'
When Henry Lennox left to catch the five o'clock train, he told her he loved her more than ever.

Later that evening, when Margaret's father said he wanted to speak to her about a very serious matter, Margaret followed him into his study

'I am going to leave Helstone,' he said.

'Why, dear Papa?'

'I'm having serious doubts about my work here,' said her father. 'I've told the bishop that I'm leaving the church. It's difficult to explain but you need to know that I suffer for my conscience.'

'What has Mother said about this?'

'She doesn't know. I'm a poor coward,' said her father. 'But she must know.'

'Where are we going?' asked Margaret.

'To Milton-Northern, an industrial town in Darkshire. I wrote to Mr Bell, my old tutor at Oxford. He suggested that I could work there as a tutor and do some real good for the people. I'll be busy and we will all forget Helstone.'

'When do we leave?' Margaret asked.

'In a fortnight,' he said. 'I'm out all day tomorrow. Will you tell your mother before I return?'

Margaret felt dizzy. 'Yes, of course,' she replied.

THINK!

Think about the value of supporting family and friends.

1 How do we know that Margaret supports Edith?

2 What problem does Margaret's father have? How does he ask Margaret to help him?

3 How do your friends support you? Do you support your friends when they need you?

The text and beyond • page 88
Values & Feelings • page 126

CHAPTER 2

Smoky Milton

The next morning was sunny and Margaret's mother seemed happier at breakfast. 'There are lots of things we can do today to help people in the village.'

Both Mr Hale and Margaret were very quiet.

Her father went out for the day. Margaret knew she had to tell her mother that they were leaving Helstone and moving north. Her father was wrong not to discuss the matter with her mother.

'Father is leaving Helstone,' Margaret said suddenly when she was walking with her mother in the garden. 'He's going to leave the church and we are going to live in Milton-Northern.'

'Don't be ridiculous!' her mother said.

'It's true. Father has doubts and because of this he can no longer remain a priest. The bishop knows. Father wrote him a letter and told him he is leaving. Father wants to become a tutor.'

Mrs Hale was shocked. 'Why does he want to live where the air is dirty and smoky, amongst factories and factory people? If he leaves

the church, no one will invite us to their homes. Why can't he be a tutor in Oxford?'

'He can't resolve[1] the doubts he has about leaving the church in Oxford,' said Margaret.

Margaret was afraid her mother might be angry when her father returned home. Mr Hale looked grey and pale. His eyes were afraid. Mrs Hale ran to him. 'Richard, you can talk to me,' she said.

In the following days, Mrs Hale became ill and Margaret and Dixon, their maid, organised the packing. They were leaving in one week, but they did not have anywhere to live in Milton.

'I have an idea,' said Margaret. 'There is a place on the sea not far from Milton called Heston. Mother and Dixon can stay there, while you and I look for a house in Milton.'

Her father agreed and Mrs Hale forgot about her illness and started looking forward to a holiday at the seaside.

---

1. resolve : find a solution to.

The house at Helstone had an echoing, empty sound once the packing cases[2] had gone to the railway station. Margaret took a last walk in the garden and thought about Henry Lennox and the moment he had asked her to marry him. So much had changed in two weeks.

They took the train to London, but everyone there was in a hurry. Heston was a restful place. Margaret liked to listen to the sound of the sea and the cries of the boys with their donkeys. She liked breathing sea air and watching the white sail of a distant boat.

The sky in Milton was a grey colour and the air tasted of smoke. They found a house where everyone would be happy. Margaret wanted the landlord to put different wallpaper in one or two of the rooms because it was horrible.

A man called Mr Thornton arrived. He was a friend of Mr Bell and had promised to help Mr Hale. He was impressed when he met

2. packing cases : 

Margaret. She was calm and beautiful and proud. Both Margaret and John were surprised when Mr Hale returned and said that the landlord would not change the wallpaper.

Margaret's mother asked about Mr Thornton when they returned to Heston that evening.

'Oh, he's about thirty,' Margaret said. 'He isn't plain or handsome. He isn't a gentleman, he's a manufacturer and he produces cotton in his factories.'

But when they moved into the house in Milton, the horrible wallpaper had gone. Mr Thornton had arranged it.

The air in Milton was smoky and Margaret felt homesick for Helstone and for London. A letter arrived from Edith telling her about their voyage across the Mediterranean. Margaret thought about her old friends.

Mr Hale liked the men he met in Milton. Several pupils knew Mr Bell and came for lessons. Mr Thornton was his favourite pupil. Mr Hale talked about things that Mr Thornton had said. Margaret's mother was jealous of their friendship.

Margaret got used to the workers in the streets at certain times of the day. The girls were friendly and they often commented on her fine clothes. One day a poorly dressed middle-aged man spoke to her. He looked tired and she smiled at him. Then one Sunday she saw him walking with his daughter. The girl looked ill. Margaret gave her some flowers and her father, who said his name was Nicholas Higgins, told her that his daughter Bessy was dying.

'I'd like to visit you.' Margaret felt shy about asking to visit someone she had only just met.

'I don't like strangers in my house,' Nicholas said, but he saw Margaret's blush and then agreed.

Milton was a brighter place for Margaret now that she had someone to care about.

THINK!

Mrs Gaskell describes Margaret as 'calm and beautiful and proud'.

1 Is pride a good or a bad feeling? Why?

2 Does Margaret feel superior to other people? Why? Why not?

3 Some people say that pride can make us want to work harder and do better. Is this true?

4 Are you a proud person? In what way?

The text and beyond • page 90
Values & Feelings • page 126

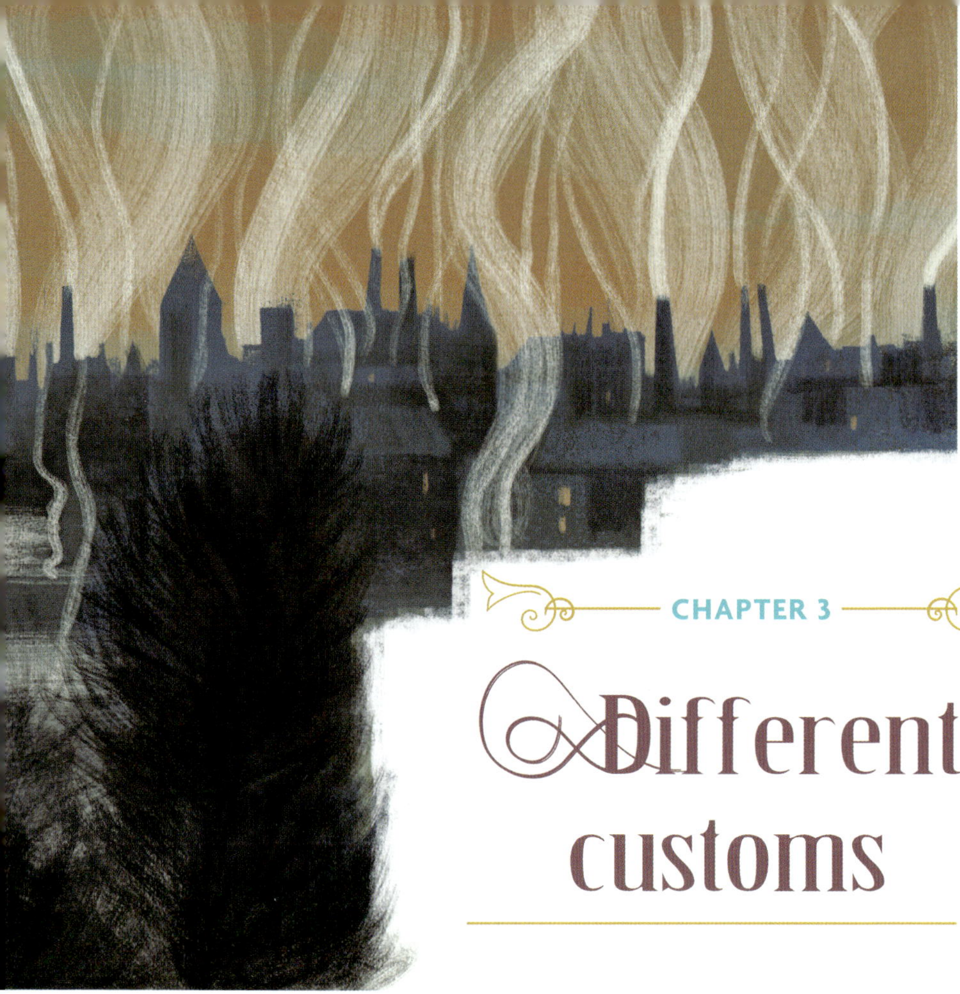

Different customs

Mrs Hale was not pleased when her husband said that Mr Thornton was coming to tea. 'Why does he want to come here?' she said.

Margaret had things she wanted to do – write a letter to Edith, read some Dante and she was irritated by her mother's complaints.

Mrs Thornton, John Thornton's mother, was a severe, dignified woman. She was also complaining. 'Why are you home early, John?' she asked her son.

'I'm having tea with Mr and Mrs Hale and Miss Margaret Hale.'

'Don't let a girl with no money try to marry you,' she warned.

John Thornton laughed. 'Margaret is polite to me but that is all. There is no danger of her wanting to marry me.'

Mrs Thornton was shocked that this girl could look down on a man like her son.

When John Thornton arrived he went into a little sitting room. Mrs Hale was sitting and Margaret was lighting the lamps for the evening. His own sitting room was bigger and grander, but it wasn't as comfortable as this one. There were pretty baskets of wood and a book lying on a table.

John Thornton watched Margaret busy with the teacups and noticed her eyes full of love for her father. Margaret looked at John Thornton, at his straight eyebrows and earnest eyes. He had beautiful teeth and a bright smile.

'I am proud to belong to this town. I would rather be working and suffering here in the north, than living a dull prosperous life in the south.'

'There is less excitement in the south,' said Margaret, 'but there is also less suffering. You don't understand the south, Mr Thornton.'

'And maybe you don't understand the north,' he said with a gentle tone in his voice.

'Well, Mr Thornton,' said Mrs Hale. 'You must admit that Milton is a smokier, dirtier town than the south.'

Mr Thornton smiled and agreed. He said the manufacturers were fair with their workers. A working man could climb to the position and power of a boss.

'So you think it's wrong for people not to improve their position,' Margaret said.

'They harm themselves. Let me explain by telling you my story.' John Thornton told them that his father died when John was only sixteen. His mother brought up John and his sister, Fanny. His mother was a strong and determined woman. She encouraged him to save

three shillings from the fifteen shillings he earned from his job. He was successful because of this and not because of luck or talent. He felt sorry for people of weak character who only liked pleasure.

When Mr Thornton left he was confused that Margaret simply bowed her head and didn't shake his hand. He thought it was rude, but in the north there were different customs[1] to the south.

'You have not met men like Mr Thornton before,' her father said.

'No,' she said.

'His father speculated, lost money and then killed himself,' Mr Hale said. 'No friends came forward to help Mrs Thornton and they were poor for a long time. When John Thornton could, he paid all the people his father had owed money to.'

'I like that,' said Margaret, 'but it is a pity that he only thinks of money.'

Margaret met Bessy Higgins in the street. She could see she was very unwell. She walked home with her. The street where they lived was poor. Bessy's younger sister, Mary, was washing clothes.

'I feel so ill.' Bessy said. 'I don't want to keep living like this.'

---

1. **customs** : traditions.

'Remember who gave you life,' Margaret said.

Bessy's father Nicholas arrived. 'Bessy's head is full of cities in the sky and golden gates. I believe only in what I can see and no more.'

Margaret held Bessy in her arms and cooled her head and face with water. She seemed to get a little better.

When Margaret returned home her father said that Mrs Thornton was visiting them the next day. Margaret wanted to visit Bessy, but she knew her mother was not strong enough to entertain a visitor alone.

Mrs Thornton didn't like weak characters. She and John were strong, but her daughter Fanny was not as strong as them. Fanny didn't want to visit the Hale family. She said she wasn't well.

'You are going with Mother.' John said. 'She needs your support.'

John Thornton hoped that the four ladies could become friends, but the visit was not a success. Mrs Thornton was offended when Margaret said she was not interested in visiting the warehouses. Neither Mrs Thornton nor Fanny wanted to visit the Hale's again.

THINK!

There are lots of contrasts in this chapter.

1   How does John contrast his home with Margaret's?

2   In what way John and Margaret contrast the north with the south? Choose from the following words:

clean   suffer   dirty   peaceful   dull   smoky   exciting   beautiful

3   Would you prefer to live in an industrial city or an agricultural village?

The text and beyond • page 92
Values & Feelings • page 126

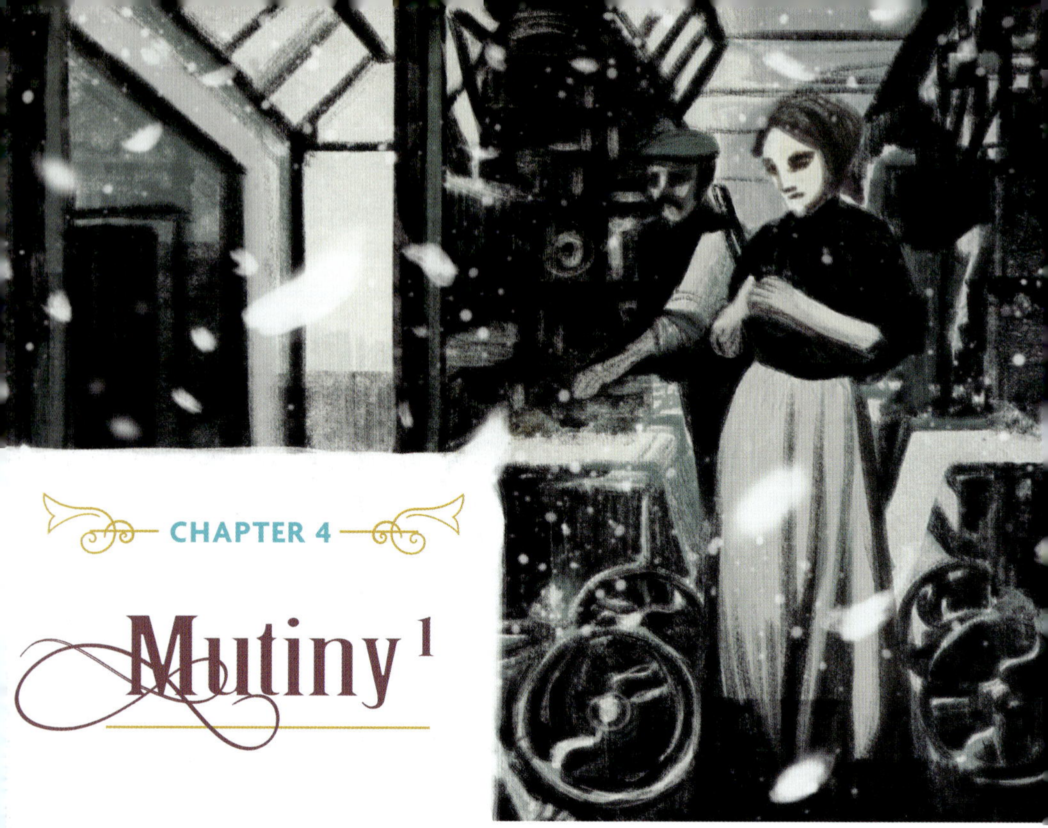

CHAPTER 4

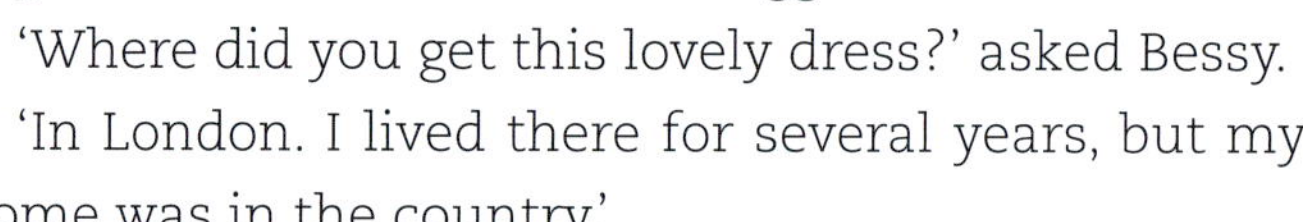

Mutiny [1]

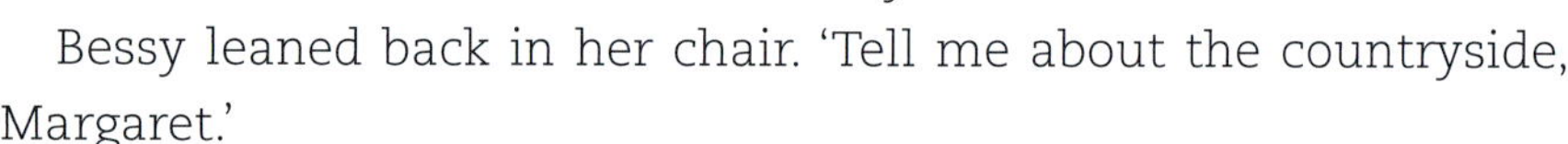

Margaret liked her visits to the Higgins house.

track 05

'Where did you get this lovely dress?' asked Bessy.

'In London. I lived there for several years, but my home was in the country.'

Bessy leaned back in her chair. 'Tell me about the countryside, Margaret.'

Margaret hadn't spoken about Helstone since she left. She described the house where they lived, the trees and the quiet with only the sound of birdsong.

'I would love to breathe clean air, but I have all this dust in my lungs. It's poisoned me.'

'Dust?' asked Margaret.

1. **mutiny :** a rebellion by sailors against a captain.

'The cotton in the factory creates a white dust. Some factories have a machine which blows it away. Not all factories can do that because it's expensive.'

'Did your father know about the white dust?'

'He did, but we worked in a good factory and he didn't want to take us somewhere else.'

'How old are you, Bessy?'

'Nineteen.'

'So am I.'

'Please, be a friend to my sister Mary, when I am no longer here,' said Bessy.

'I will,' said Margaret.

It was a year since they first arrived in Milton.

Margaret was worried about her mother's ill health. Her father said there was nothing to worry about, but Margaret knew he was worried.

One evening Mrs Hale spoke to Margaret about her brother Frederick.

'You can see from his letters, that Fredcrick didn't

like Captain Reid. None of the sailors did. He was cruel and unfair. That's why the sailors rose up in mutiny and took control of the ship *The Orion*.'

'Mutiny?' said Margaret.

'Yes, they put the Captain and a few other sailors in a little boat.'

'Was Frederick one of the sailors who took control of *The Orion*?'

'Yes. He escaped but some of the sailors were court martialled.'[2]

'What happened to them, Mother?'

'They were hanged.[3] And now Frederick is in Cádiz. He has changed his name to Dickenson and he can never come home.'

The next day when Margaret was walking to Mr Thornton's house with her father, he told her he was worried about his wife.

'I am afraid that the air in Milton is killing your mother. We can ask Mrs Thornton if she knows a good doctor.'

The Thorntons lived close to the mill in a beautiful stone house that was blackened by smoke.

---

2. were court martialled : went in front of a military court.
3. hanged : killed. Suspended from a rope.

It was noisy and the sitting rooms looked onto the factory yard. The house was clean but not comfortable.

'I was sorry John couldn't come to his lesson yesterday,' Mr Hale said when Mrs Thornton arrived.

'He is busy. He doesn't have time to study the classics.'

'I respect and admire him,' said Margaret. 'I have heard good things about John.'

'Who has spoken to you about him?' Mrs Thornton asked.

'Mr Bell,' said Margaret.

Later that evening Mr Thornton visited Margaret and her family. He had the name of a good doctor and he wanted to talk about problems he had at the mill.

'The workers think that business is as good as last year but it isn't. They want a five per cent rise, but I may have to lower their wages.'

'And then what will happen?' asked Margaret.

'The workers will strike and you will see Milton without smoke.'

'It is silly for workers and employers to argue when they are dependent on one another,' said Margaret.

'The workers are like children, Margaret,' said John Thornton. 'They need a firm hand to guide them.'

'You are holding a lot of power over a group of men. This power brings great responsibility.'

'I understand what you are saying,' said John Thornton. 'I am responsible for them during work hours, but after work I respect their independence.'

Once again Margaret did not shake his hand. John Thornton thought she was too proud.

When Dr Donaldson visited Mrs Hale, Margaret asked him what was the matter with her mother. The doctor told her that things were not good. Margaret grew pale. Mrs Hale was tearful.

'I shall never see Helstone again, or Frederick, my first born child.'

Margaret and Dixon put her mother to bed.

'Don't tell your father this terrible news,' said Dixon.

'I won't.' Margaret gave Dixon a big kiss and ran from the room.

'Bless[4] her,' said Dixon. 'The three people I love are Mrs Hale, Frederick and Margaret. That's all.'

---

4. bless : ask God to protect.

THINK!

Frederick's exile doesn't seem fair.

1 Why did the sailors rise up in mutiny?

2 What happened to the sailors who were court martialled?

3 It doesn't seem fair that Mrs Hale becomes very unwell in Milton. What will she never see again?

4 Do you know of a situation that wasn't fair? Talk about it.

The text and beyond • page 94
Values & Feelings • page 126

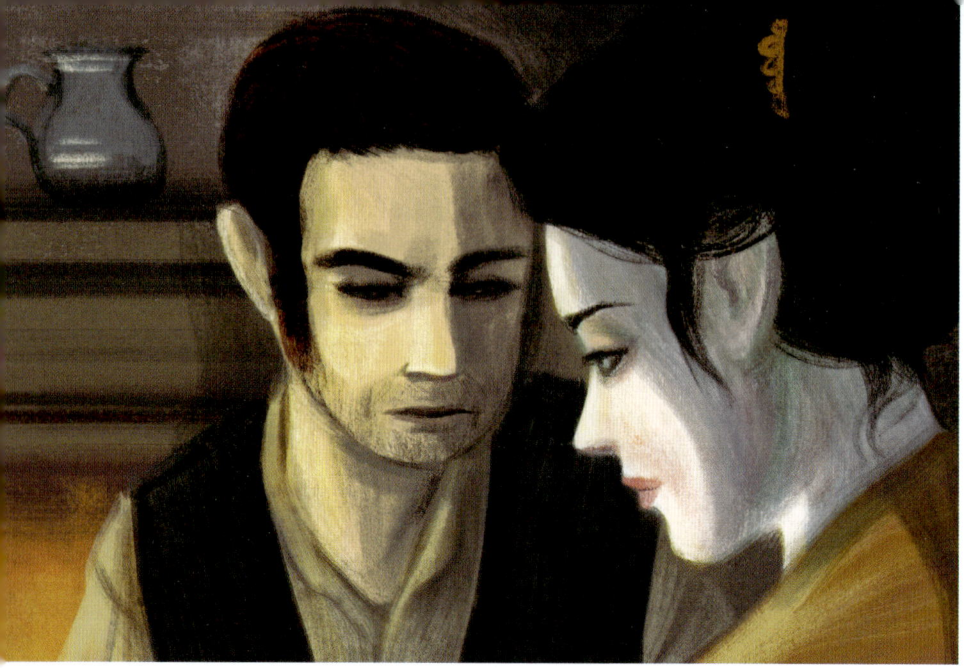

CHAPTER 5

Strike and starvation

Nicholas sat staring into the fire. 'I don't like this strike,' he said to Margaret. 'But the mill owners will soon ask us to come back to work.'

track 06

'They don't strike in the south,' said Margaret. 'If the farm workers stopped work there would be no seed sown[1] and nothing would grow. What would happen to the farmers?'

'They'd have to give up their farms,' said Nicholas. 'Or pay the right wage.'

1. **sewn :** to plant a seed.

'And supposing they couldn't pay?' said Margaret.

'I know the ways of the north, not the south,' said Nicholas.

'Why are you striking?' asked Margaret.

'Because the mills are doing well and getting richer. The mill owners want the workers to take less, but we won't.'

'And so you get your revenge by dying.'

'You are a foreigner,' said Nicholas. 'You don't know the ways of the north. We make profits for the mill owners and we want to help them spend the money. John Thornton is a stubborn man.'

'Poor Bessy,' said Margaret. 'You don't want to listen to all this fighting.'

'It's alright for you,' Bessy said to Margaret when her father had gone out. 'You have a good life. You don't have any worries.'

Margaret looked at her. 'Oh, I do, Bessy,' she said in a small voice. 'My mother is ill. She's dying, Bessy, and my father doesn't know. The person who can comfort my mother is falsely accused of a crime. He risks death if he comes home. My life is not what it seems.'

'I'm so sorry,' said Bessy.

'I must go, but telling you has made me feel better.'

'I have never met anyone like you before,' said Bessy.

Two letters were on the table when Margaret returned home. One was from Aunt Shaw, who was on holiday in Italy. The other was from Mrs Thornton inviting them all for dinner. Mrs Hale was too weak and unwell, but she insisted that her husband and Margaret go.

That evening John Thornton asked his mother who was coming to the dinner.

'Mr Hale and his daughter, but Mrs Hale can't because she's unwell,' said Mrs Thornton. 'Mrs Hale is *always* unwell. Miss Hale thinks she is more important than she really is. They are not a rich family.'

'And Margaret can't play the piano,' said Fanny.

'I want you to like Miss Hale,' John Thornton said.

His mother looked surprised. 'Are you thinking of marrying a girl with no money, John?'

'She wouldn't accept me if I asked her,' said John.

'No, I don't think she would,' said his mother, 'but she won't find a better man.'

'I am tired of talking about Miss Hale,' said Fanny.

'Let us talk about the strike then,' said John. 'My men are still working at the mill because they don't want to break their contracts. The workers do not realise that we are in competition with the Americans who are selling cotton at a cheaper price.'

'Can you get workers from Ireland?' asked Mrs Thornton.

'Yes, I can. The men in Milton will be sorry if they lose their jobs.'

Bessy was surprised that Margaret had been invited to the Thornton's.

'They are wealthy. Visitors from Parliament have dinner with them.'

Margaret smiled. 'We're not rich, Bessy, but we're educated and that is why we're accepted into society.'

'What will you wear?' asked Bessy.

'I will wear a beautiful white silk dress. I wore it to my cousin's wedding.' Margaret was silent. 'Is your father on strike, Bessy?'

'He is.'

Then the door opened and Nicholas came in. Margaret got up. She told Bessy she wanted to see her before she went to the Thornton's for dinner.

'You can tell Mr Thornton that soon he will have no workers to complete his work,' said Nicholas. 'If I was having dinner with him I would talk to him about money.'

Margaret said nothing and returned home. The next time she visited Bessy, a neighbour called Mr Boucher was there.

'My family is starving. I can't go on with this strike much longer,' said Mr Boucher.

'Don't give in,' said Nicholas. 'Take food from here. I'll help you.'

Mr Boucher's face was white and thin and hopeless. When he left, Margaret was silent. She took her purse and gave all the money she had to Bessy.

When Margaret told her mother about Mr Boucher and his family, Mrs Hale told Margaret to pack a basket with food.

'Is it wrong to help these men?' Mrs Hale asked her husband.

'You are right to send food,' said Mr Hale, 'but the answer to the problem is for the men to return to work.'

On the night of the dinner party Margaret looked lovely. Her thick black hair was arranged on her head. She wore her white silk dress and a coral necklace. She was sad that her mother could not see the beautiful dining table.

John Thornton shook hands with Margaret. It was the first time their hands had met.

She looked beautiful and he loved her red lips and the way her head bent forwards when she talked to someone. He did not go near Margaret for the rest of the evening and she began to notice him. She liked his dignified manner and she could see that his friends liked his strong character.

Margaret enjoyed the dinner party and John Thornton's friends asked who the beautiful and elegant woman was.

THINK!

Think about the characters' feelings of prejudice in this chapter.

1 How does Bessy imagine Margaret's life to be like?

2 Why is Bessy surprised that Margaret is invited to the Thornton's for dinner?

3 How does Margaret explain her position in society?

4 What prejudices does Mrs Thornton have about Margaret?

The text and beyond • page 96
Values & Feelings • page 126

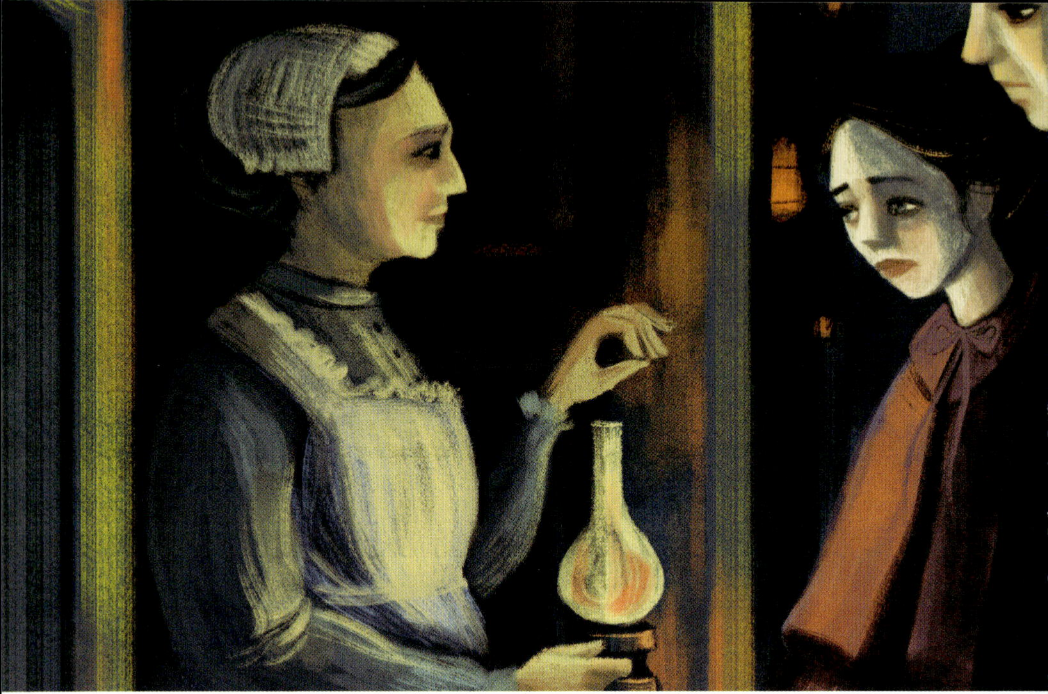

CHAPTER 6

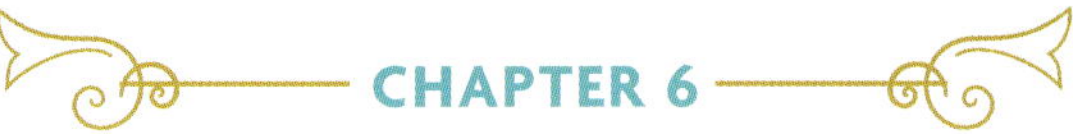

Trouble at the mill

Margaret and her father spoke about the interesting evening, but their smiles changed when Dixon opened the door.

track 07

'Thank goodness you are home,' she said. 'I thought Mrs Hale was going to die, but Dr Donaldson is here now.'

Mr Hale was shocked. He did not know his wife was so unwell. 'Will she get better?' he asked Dr Donaldson.

'She will be fine tonight and for a few days but Mrs Hale will not get better.'

Margaret sat all night at her mother's bedside. The next day she decided to ask Mrs Thornton if they could borrow her waterbed.[1] It would be more comfortable for Mrs Hale. It was August and the weather was hot. People were standing and talking on the road to the mill. The atmosphere was dark and angry. When Margaret arrived at the house, she realised that there was no sound from the machines. The mill was silent.

John Thornton had brought workers from Ireland and the people of Milton were very angry. The Irish workers were afraid of the angry crowd. They were eating and sleeping inside the mill. The crowd were trying to force their way through the gates to the mill.

'I'm sorry, Miss Hale, that you are here at such a bad moment,' said John Thornton. 'The soldiers will be here in twenty minutes.'

'These people don't need soldiers,' Margaret said to him. 'They need you to speak to them.'

John went out of the house to speak to the crowd and Margaret looked out of the window. She saw John standing with his arms folded, still as a statue.

Many in the crowd were boys, cruel and thoughtless and there were men who looked like angry wolves.

Margaret saw Mr Boucher, mad with rage.

The crowd turned towards the mill door which was where the frightened Irish workers were hiding. She saw boys taking off their heavy wooden shoes ready to throw them. She was afraid for John Thornton, so she went outside and stood at his side.

'The soldiers are coming,' she said to the crowd. 'Go home.'

Someone in the crowd asked if the Irish workers would be sent away. When John Thornton said 'No,' the crowd went wild.

---

1. waterbed : a bed with a mattress full of water.

The crowd became angrier and Margaret put her arms around John Thornton to protect him. One of the boys threw a stone and it hit Margaret on the head. She fainted.

'You are here to hurt innocent strangers and now you attack a woman,' he said to them.

'The stone was meant for you,' shouted a boy. 'You're a coward to stand behind a woman.'

John Thornton was angry. He walked towards the crowd. 'Now, kill me.'

But the crowd moved away.

Fanny was upset when the servants told her what had happened to Margaret. The servants also told Fanny how Margaret had put her arms around John to protect him.

'Margaret would like to marry my brother,' she said to the servants, 'but he will never marry her.'

Margaret heard her say this and felt ashamed. She decided to go home.

John Thornton was disappointed that Margaret had left. 'I must thank her for what she did,' he said to his mother.

'It proves that she loves you,' his mother said.

'I have to ask Miss Hale something,' John said. 'I don't know if she cares for me the way I care for her, but I have to find out.'

'Go tomorrow,' said his mother and then she went to her room and cried tears of jealousy.

Margaret was a proud woman. She felt embarrassed that so many people had seen her with her arms around John Thornton.

She was angry with herself that she had been so impulsive. When Margaret saw John Thornton she was nervous and worried.

'I want to thank you,' he said. 'You saved my life yesterday. I realise that I love you.'

'This is terrible,' said Margaret. 'A real gentleman would understand that I was only trying to protect you. I didn't do it because I'm in love with you.'

'I had to tell you how I feel,' he said. 'I'll always love you even if you don't love me.'

When John Thornton left, Margaret saw tears in his eyes. She felt sad that she had caused him so much pain.

In Margaret's young life, two men had told her that they loved her. She and Henry Lennox had been friends, but she had never considered John Thornton a friend. Their conversations had often ended in disagreement and the sudden knowledge that he loved her frightened Margaret.

There were lots of people in Milton who were worried. Bessy was worried she wouldn't see Margaret again. Nicholas Higgins was upset about the riot.[2] Mrs Hale was worried that she would not see Frederick again before she died. She asked Margaret to write to him and ask him to come home. Margaret sent the letter and then told her father what she had done.

'It's very dangerous for Frederick to come here, but you have done the right thing,' Mr Hale said.

They were all scared of the punishment for mutineers.

---

2. riot : a violent disturbance.

THINK!

Margaret demonstrates in this chapter that she is a strong woman.

1   How do we know that she is a strong woman?
2   Are there other strong women in this chapter? Who?
3   Are you strong when there is a difficult situation? How?

The text and beyond • page 98
Values & Feelings • page 126

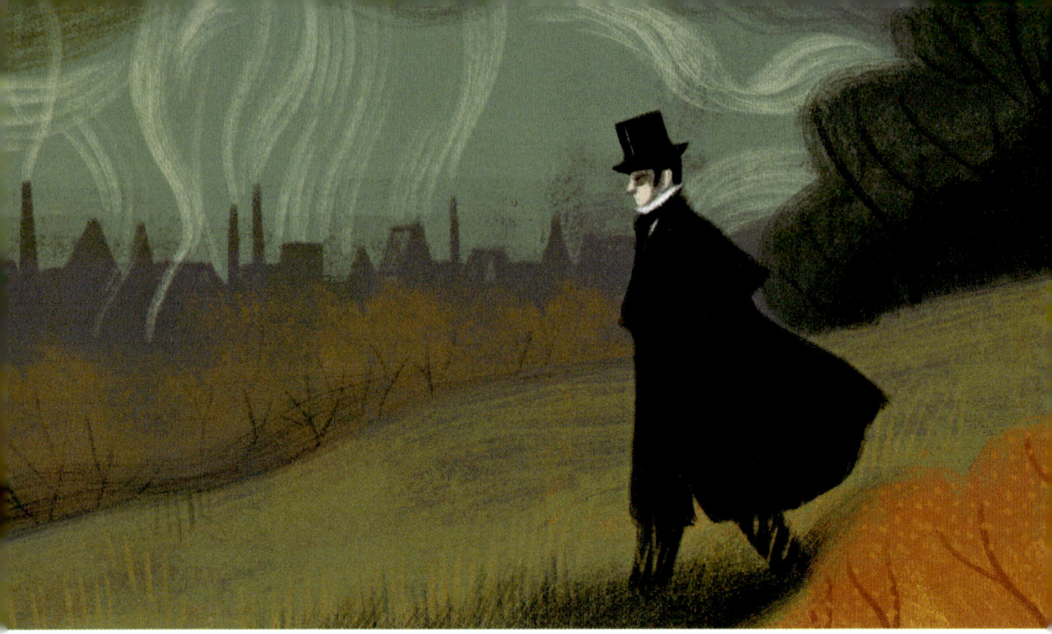

CHAPTER 7

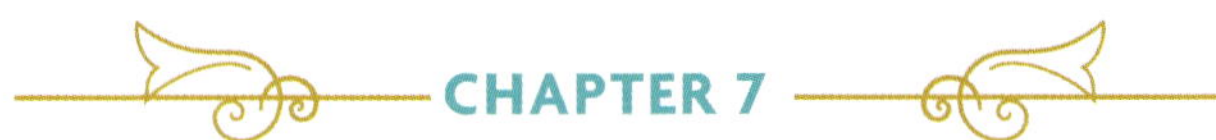

A mother's love

John Thornton had a headache. He could not bear noise or light. He felt foolish because he could do nothing about the love he felt for Margaret. He went for a long ride into the country but even the fresh air did not change his feelings.

track 08

His mother waited anxiously at home for news of his engagement. 'Well, John?' she said when he finally arrived.

'No one loves me. Only you care for me, Mother.'

'You are right,' she said. 'A mother's love is strong, but a girl's love is like a puff of smoke.'

'I am not good enough for her, Mother.'

'Nonsense. I hate that girl.'

'Don't hate her,' said John. They did not mention Margaret again.

The next day John Thornton was busy with matters concerning the strike. He met Dr Donaldson in the street and when John asked about Mrs Hale, the doctor told him she only had a few weeks to live.

'Can I do anything?' John asked.

'She loves pears,' said the doctor.

'Then I will buy her some,' said John.

John Thornton decided to deliver the pears to Mrs Hale, but he only stayed for a moment.

'How kind of him to think of me,' said Mrs Hale.

Margaret agreed but said little. When she went to her room she found Dixon searching for something.

'I don't like to be the person to tell you this,' said Dixon, 'but that young girl you visit, Bessy, died this morning. Her sister Mary is downstairs. Bessy asked to be buried in one of your nightcaps.'

Margaret cried when she saw Mary and even though she didn't want to go to the house, she went that afternoon. Bessy's face, which had been full of pain, had the soft smile of eternal rest. She looked more peaceful in death than in life.

Her father Nicholas cried when he knew Bessy had died.

'Come home with me,' said Margaret. 'My father used to be a priest and he can help at times like this.'

Nicholas walked home with Margaret and soon he began talking earnestly with Mr Hale. 'The people of Darkshire think about real things like money and food. They don't have time to think about eternal life.'

Nicholas talked to Mr Hale about the strike and the mistakes that the workers had made. The rioters brought the strike to an end but in a shameful[1] way and Nicholas was angry with the Milton workers who did not obey the Union.

'Is the strike over?' asked Margaret.

'Yes, it is. Most workers are ready to go back to work, but my boss, Hamper, thinks I'm a troublemaker. He won't give me a job.'

'I wish you would talk to the bosses,' said Mr Hale. 'Talking is the best way to solve problems. What about talking to John Thornton?'

'Thornton! He brought the Irish workers here. He didn't punish the rioters.'

'He thought losing their jobs was enough punishment,' said Margaret. 'But tell me, Nicholas, how does the Union work?'

'If a man doesn't belong to the Union, then the people who work with him are not allowed to speak to him.'

'That's torture,'[2] said Margaret. 'The Unions are worse than the bosses.'

Nicholas didn't agree, but it was late and time to go home. Before he left all three of them said a prayer for Bessy.

---

1. **shameful :** bringing disgrace.
2. **torture :** cause severe physical pain.

The next day a letter arrived from Edith telling them about her son and about the happy life she was leading. Edith wanted Margaret to visit Corfu and bring her mother. Edith was sure that the warm weather and clean air would be good for Mrs Hale. Margaret wanted to live just one day like Edith. She had no worries, a lovely home and blue skies.

Margaret and Mrs Hale were sure that Frederick would receive their letter soon and come to Milton.

'When Frederick is here we must keep our doors shut and let no one in,' said Margaret. 'We can send Martha, the maid, on holiday and Mary Higgins, Bessy's sister, can work here.'

John Thornton continued to visit the Hale family. He brought fruit but he didn't try to speak to Margaret. His eyes were cold. He was offended and Margaret felt sad that she had hurt him. Even though it was painful, John was happy to be in the same room as Margaret.

THINK!

Look at the sentence below taken from this chapter.
'No one loves me. Only you care for me, Mother.'

1 We feel John Thornton's pain. Why? What has happened?

2 Why is Margaret sad in this chapter?

3 Has there been a time when you felt sad?

The text and beyond • page 100
Values & Feelings • page 126

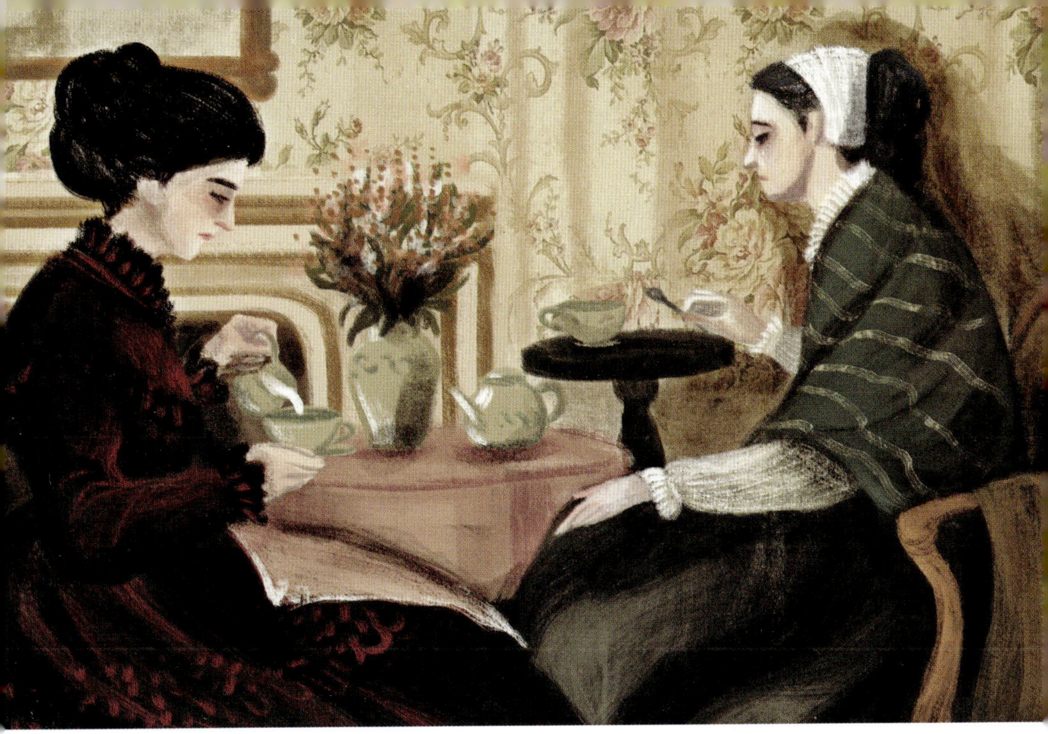

CHAPTER 8

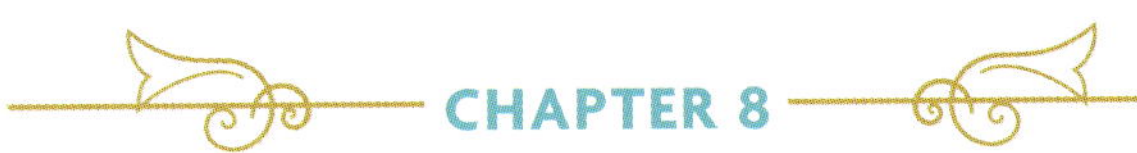

Frederick

Mrs Hale was much worse when Mrs Thornton came to see her. She didn't believe John when he said that Mrs Hale was very unwell. She realised she had been wrong. They were both mothers and Mrs Hale was the younger woman.

track 09

'My child will be without a mother. My sister is in Italy. There is no one else. If I die...' Mrs Hale's voice stopped.

Mrs Thornton thought of her daughter, a small child, who had died many years ago. 'You want me to be a friend to Miss Hale,' she said.

Mrs Hale pressed Mrs Thornton's hand. She couldn't speak.

'I can't give her lots of affection,' said Mrs Thornton, 'but I will be a friend to Miss Hale.'

'Call her Margaret,' said Mrs Hale. 'Thank you for your promise of kindness to my child.'

Later, Dixon sat with Mrs Hale. The house was still and quiet and then the front doorbell rang. Margaret opened the door. A tall man stood there.

'Frederick!' She took his hands and pulled him into the house.

'Oh, Margaret,' Frederick said. 'How is Mother?'

'She's very ill, but alive,' said Margaret and went to find her father. 'Papa, guess who's here?'

When Mr Hale knew it was Frederick he began to cry like a child. Margaret took her father to the study where Frederick was waiting, but she could not bear to see them meet after so long. She ran upstairs to her room and cried for the first time in days. The strain[1] of the past months had been terrible, but Frederick had arrived. Margaret could share the responsibility with him.

'I don't believe Mother is going to die,' said Frederick. 'She needs a London doctor to examine her.'

'It wouldn't do any good,' said Margaret.

'We must do everything we can,' said Frederick.

Frederick sat with his mother all night and at breakfast talked to his father about the life he had led in South America and Mexico,

---

1. **strain** : pressure.

before settling in Cádiz. Mrs Hale became much worse during the day. By evening she was unconscious and before morning came she was dead. Frederick cried violently but Mr Hale could not cry. He sat talking to his wife and stroking[2] her face.

It was a chill October and Margaret was busy looking after her father and brother and arranging the funeral.

One evening Dixon spoke to Margaret. 'I'm worried about Frederick's safety,' she said. 'I met a man called Leonards. He was on the ship *The Orion* at the same time as Master Frederick. Leonards told me that Master Frederick will hang for mutiny if they ever catch him. He said there is a hundred pounds reward and if I help him catch Master Frederick he will give me half of this money.'

'Have you told Frederick?' said Margaret.

'No, I haven't.'

'Then, I will,' said Margaret.

'You must go, Frederick,' Mr Hale said when he heard.

'Leonards is a dangerous man,' said Frederick. 'But I wish I could stay and clear my name. There is a girl I'm in love with. Her name is Dolores Barbour and I would like you to meet her.'

'I think you should fight the charges against you,' said Margaret. 'You could speak to a lawyer I know. Mr Henry Lennox is in London. You could take the night train to London tomorrow evening.'

Margaret travelled with Frederick to the station. Frederick told her he was worried that their father looked weak and if he died then Margaret would be all alone.

'Think about the present,' she said. 'We shall write often to one another.'

---

2. stroking : gently touching.

Margaret saw Mr Thornton at the station, but she did not speak to him. As Margaret and Frederick were walking along the platform, an aggressive looking man pushed Margaret to one side. He took Frederick by the collar. 'Your name is Hale!' he said.

Frederick pulled away from the man who had been drinking. The man fell off the side of the platform. He landed by the side of the railroad.

'Run,' shouted Margaret, 'The train is here.'

'Bless you, Margaret.' Then the train and her brother were gone.

Margaret overheard some railway officials talking to each other about a man called Leonards. He asked to borrow some money so he could buy a train ticket to London. Margaret was afraid as she walked back that she might meet Leonards, but she didn't.

The house was quiet and Mr Hale was sad that Mr Bell could not come to the funeral. He wanted Mr Thornton to accompany him, but Margaret would not let him.

'Let me go with you,' she said.

'Women don't go to funerals.'

'I will be no trouble, Father.'

Then a letter arrived from Frederick telling them that Mr Lennox was out of town. He was staying in London for a few more days.

Margaret saw Nicholas and his daughter Mary at the funeral, but she did not see John Thornton. He was there standing at the back. He was wondering who the handsome young man was with Margaret that night. She had looked so happy with him. It caused John great pain.

John Thornton was visiting Mr Hale, when Margaret was called downstairs.

'There's a police inspector to see you,' said Dixon.

'Don't let my father come down,' said Margaret.

The police inspector was surprised by Margaret's proud manner. She did not ask any questions but waited for him to speak.

'A man died in hospital because of a fall at the station on Thursday evening.'

Margaret didn't tremble. She looked at him steadily.

'An eye witness said that you were with a young gentleman and he pushed the man over the edge of the platform.'

'I was not there,' said Margaret.

'So, you were not at the station with a young man who pushed another man and caused his death.'

'I was not there,' Margaret repeated.

Her repetition made the Inspector suspicious.

'May I call on you again?'

Margaret bowed her head as they went towards the door.

She kept her eyes on the inspector until he left the house.

Margaret locked the door and then collapsed on the floor.

THINK!

Frederick risks capture by the police when he travels to Milton.

1 Why does he come to Milton? What does this tell us about Frederick?

2 How does Margaret show her loyalty to Frederick?

3 Do you think family loyalty is important? Why?

The text and beyond • page 102
Values & Feelings • page 126

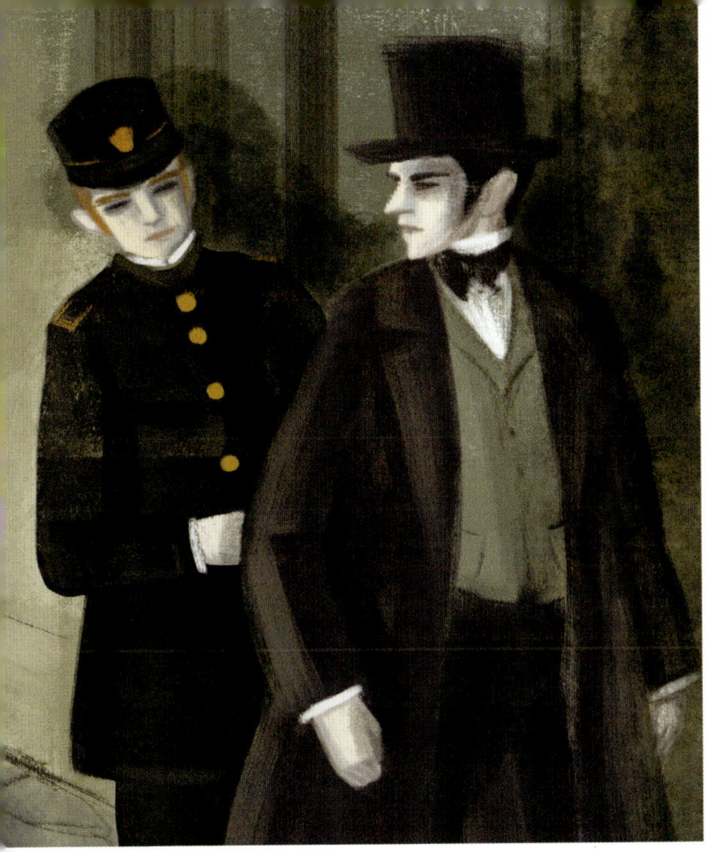

CHAPTER 9

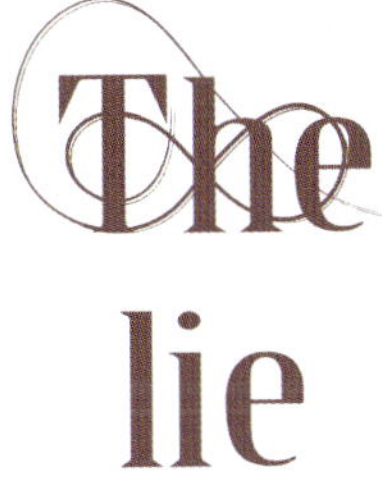

The lie

Margaret wondered why she was lying on the ground. She sat up and then she remembered. She told a lie to the police inspector. That was terrible, but the lie had saved Frederick.

track 10

When John Thornton left the Hale's, he met the police inspector.

'You are the magistrate who saw Leonards on his death bed,' the police inspector said to him.

'Yes, I am,' said John Thornton.

'You are a friend of the Hales. We think that a gentleman who was walking with Miss Hale at the station pushed Leonards off the platform and caused his death. The young lady says she wasn't there. I have a witness who thinks it was her, but he is not completely sure.'

'Come to my warehouse in an hour,' said Thornton.

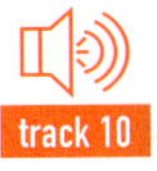

John Thornton hurried to his office to think. Margaret had told a lie, but he had to save her from shame. He wrote a note to the police inspector.

There will be no inquest because there's insufficient medical evidence. No further action is needed. I will take full responsibility.

The police officer was pleased when he read this. He returned to the house to speak to Margaret.

'Mr Thornton has said there will be no inquest.' The police officer showed Margaret the note.

Margaret thanked him and said goodnight. Then she lay on her bed. John Thornton saw her with Frederick that night at the station. She valued his respect and she felt ashamed.[1] He now knew she was a liar.

Margaret was pleased when a letter arrived from Frederick. He had met Mr Lennox and discussed the court martial. Frederick had to find witnesses before Henry Lennox could continue with the case.[2] Frederick was now in Spain.

When Margaret and her father visited Nicholas Higgins, he was still at home – there was no work for him. He couldn't ask his old employer Hamper for work, because Hamper wouldn't allow his workers to be members of the Union.

'Mr Boucher said the Union does more harm than good,' said Margaret gently.

'The Union means strength,' said Nicholas. 'Workers will only get their rights[3] through being part of the Union. Boucher caused a lot of trouble and Hamper won't give him a job. Now Boucher has run away.'

'Poor Mr Boucher,' said Margaret. 'You shouldn't have made him join the Union.'

1. **ashemed :** sorry.
2. **case :** (here) a dispute in court.
3. **rights :** morally or legally allowed to have.

They heard a sound outside in the street. Six men were carrying a door and lying on the door was a dead man.

'John Boucher drowned,' someone said.

Margaret covered his face with a handkerchief.

The men asked Nicholas to tell Mr Boucher's wife, but he shook his head. It was Margaret who told his wife the terrible news.

'He's left me alone with all these children,' Mrs Boucher said. 'Six children and the oldest is nearly eight years old.'

Margaret and her father stopped at Nicholas Higgins' door before they went home. They knocked but he didn't want to speak.

Margaret wanted to see Mr Thornton again. When the doorbell rang and it wasn't him, she felt disappointed. It was Nicholas Higgins. Mr Hale asked Dixon to bring some tea and when they were alone, he spoke to Mr Hale.

'I feel responsible for Bucher's widow and children. I want to help them. Maybe I can find work in the south?'

Margaret came into the room. 'I don't think that's a good idea. You would have to work on the land in all weather and you are not used to that. Ask Mr Thornton for work.'

'I can write him a note,' said Mr Hale.

'Thank you, sir, but I don't need any help.'

When Nicholas left, Mr Hale said to Margaret what a proud man he was. Margaret hoped that John Thornton would listen to him with his human heart and not his Master's ears.

John Thornton often thought about the fond look Margaret had given the young man at the station. He was jealous of the dark, thin, elegant stranger. John was irritable at work and silent at home.

One day his mother asked to speak to him about their servant Betsy. 'She wants to leave because her lover's death has made her sad. The night he died a young man walking with Miss Hale pushed him.'

'Leonards was not killed by a push,' said John.

'Other people saw Miss Hale out that night. I promised her mother I would look after her.'

'I believe the young man is her lover,' said John.

'Then I must speak to her.'

'You have been seen out in the evening with a young man,' Mrs Thornton said when she arrived at the house.

'Whatever your son has said about me is incorrect,' said Margaret.

'My son has said nothing. If Fanny was out with a young man at night, I would be very worried.'

'I can give you no explanation,' said Margaret. 'I'm sorry but I'm going to leave the room.'

Higgins met Thornton on the street. 'I must speak to you, sir. My name is Higgins.'

John Thornton knew about Higgins's role in the strike. 'What do you want, Mr Higgins?'

'I want work. I have to care for John Boucher's widow and children.'

'I won't give you work,' said Thornton. He watched the man walk away. He asked the porter how long Higgins had been waiting.

'Five hours,' said the porter.

THINK!

Look at the sentence below taken from this chapter.

She sat up and then she remembered. She told a lie to the police inspector.

1   Why does Margaret tell a lie? Is she wrong to do this?

2   Is there a time when a 'white lie' is important?

3   How do you feel if you ever tell a lie?

The text and beyond • page 104
Values & Feelings • page 126

 Mr Bell's visit

It was clear to Margaret that John Thornton and his mother thought the man she was with at the station was her lover.  She did not know what to do. Margaret felt that she had passed from childhood to old age in just one year and she knew she would never marry. Why was she always so proud? Why hadn't she behaved differently with John Thornton?

That afternoon she visited Mrs Boucher who was very unwell. Nicholas was there playing with the little children.

'Did Mr Thornton give you a job?' asked Margaret.

'He didn't,' said Nicholas.

'I'm sorry. I'm very disappointed,' said Margaret.

There was a sound behind them and when they turned round, John Thornton was standing there. Margaret bowed her head and left the cottage while Thornton spoke to Nicholas Higgins.

'So, these are Mr Boucher's children you told me about,' said John Thornton.'I am sorry that I didn't believe you when you spoke about them. I would like you to work for me.'

Nicholas thought about it for a moment and then said, 'I will.' The two men shook hands.

When John Thornton left, he met Margaret on the road and told her that he had given Higgins a job. Margaret said she was glad and then the conversation turned to the subject of truth. Margaret wanted to explain everything to John Thornton but she had to remain loyal to Frederick.

'I won't ask any questions,' said John Thornton, 'and you mustn't worry because I'm not in love with you anymore.'

'I know you're not,' said Margaret. 'You must understand that I can't tell another person's secret or explain it, without causing them harm.'

Margaret seemed unnaturally happy when she returned home, but later in the evening there were tears in her eyes. Her father told her that Mr Bell, his old friend from Oxford, was coming to visit, but Margaret was more interested in a letter from Aunt Shaw. She was returning to her London home in Harley Street and Captain Lennox and Edith were returning to England.

Margaret and Mr Bell liked each other immediately. Mr Bell enjoyed teasing her. He said she was a democrat[1] and a socialist[2] and it was because she lived in the north.

'Everyone in Milton is in a hurry to make money,' said Mr Bell. 'No one sits still.'

'And I expect the people of Milton think that people from Oxford are lazy,' said Margaret.

John Thornton came to the house to meet Mr Bell. He still loved

---

1. **democrat :** someone who believes in equality.
2. **socialist :** a system of government ownership.

Margaret and when he overheard Mr Hale say that 'a letter from Mr
Lennox had made Margaret hopeful,' he felt very jealous. He became
irritable and misunderstood Mr Bell's jokes. He was uncomfortable
when they spoke about the strike. Margaret changed the subject to
her cousin Edith. She said the shawls[3] were better and cheaper in
Corfu than in London.

'That can't be true,' said Mr Hale.

'Is Miss Hale always so truthful?' said John Thornton. He regretted
saying this as soon as the words were spoken. He didn't understand
why he had been so cruel. Margaret sat quite still and he saw her
body tremble.

Mr Bell noticed everything and once he and Mr Hale were alone,
he suggested that Thornton and Margaret were in love. Mr Hale had
not noticed, but he became curious. One day he asked Margaret if
Mr Thornton cared for her.

3. shawl : 

'Yes, I think so,' she said.

'And you refused him?'

She gave a long sigh. 'Yes.'

There was silence for a minute. Mr Hale stroked Margaret's cheek and found that it was wet with tears.

March brought news of Frederick's marriage to Dolores and there were letters from Henry Lennox. He didn't think that Frederick could defend himself at a court martial. Frederick's letters were angry. He said he wouldn't live in England if he had permission to return. This made Margaret cry. Her plans for Frederick had failed.

Mr Hale was not well that spring. Margaret was happy when he decided to accept an invitation to stay with Mr Bell in Oxford. Margaret could do what she wanted. She chatted to their maid Martha about Fanny Thornton's marriage to a rich older gentleman. She read Henry Lennox's letters about Frederick and she thought about John Thornton.

Mr Hale was enjoying his visit to Oxford, but he felt very tired.

'I'm fifty-five years old,' he said to Mr Bell.

'That's young. I'm over sixty,' said Mr Bell.

'If I die, what will happen to Margaret?'

'I will always take care of Margaret,' said Mr Bell.

The next morning, when the servant went into Mr Hale's room to wake him, he did not answer. Mr Hale had died during the night.

Mr Bell was shocked and caught the next train to Milton. Mr Thornton was on the same train and the two men sat together.

'I'm going to Milton to tell Margaret that her father has died,' said Mr Bell. 'He came to stay with me in Oxford.'

'How shocking! What will Margaret do?' said Thornton.

'I will look after her, but there are also those Lennoxes.'

'Who are they?' said Thornton.

'They are smart London people. Captain Lennox married Margaret's cousin Edith. Henry Lennox, the captain's brother, is a lawyer and he will want to marry Margaret now that she will have my money when I die.'

Margaret saw Mr Bell arrive and understood immediately. 'I can tell from your face what has happened. Oh, Papa!'

Margaret did not cry, but lay on the sofa with her eyes shut and didn't speak.

'Can Mrs Lennox come and stay with her?' asked Mr Bell.

'She is about to have another baby,' said Dixon. 'And Aunt Shaw won't want to leave Edith.'

'Nonsense,' said Mr Bell. He wrote a letter to Aunt Shaw telling her to come to Milton.

Mr Bell was invited to stay at the Thornton's until he returned to Oxford. John was sad when he heard that Margaret was going to live in London. The last eighteen months had been painful and wonderful.

'How is Miss Hale?' asked Mrs Thornton.

'Broken,' said Mr Bell, 'but her relatives are here now.'

'Where have these relatives been?' asked Mrs Thornton.

'They were living abroad. Aunt Shaw brought Margaret up. Her cousin Edith is like a sister to her. There's also Frederick.'

'Who is Frederick?' asked John.

'Her brother. He was involved in a mutiny and now has to live in Spain. He would be arrested if he set foot in England,' said Mr Bell.

'Was he here at the time when Mrs Hale died?' John asked.

'I don't think so,' said Mr Bell.

'I saw a young man walking with Miss Hale,'

'That would be Henry Lennox,' said Mr Bell.

'But tell me, I thought you liked Margaret?'

'She's a beautiful creature,'

said John Thornton.

'That is like a description of a horse,'

said Mr Bell.

Mr Thornton's eyes glowed.

His feelings for Margaret were as strong as ever but he would not admit them to Mr Bell.

He could not tell Mr Bell how much he loved Margaret.

THINK!

It's obvious that John Thornton is jealous when Mr Bell speaks about Henry Lennox.

1 Why hasn't Margaret told John about Frederick?

2 Mr Bell knows that John Thornton loves Margaret. How do we know this?

3 Can you remember a time when you felt jealous? Why?

The text and beyond • page 106
Values & Feelings • page 126

Inheritance

Aunt Shaw did not like Milton because it was noisy and smoky. She thought her niece looked pale and ill and she wanted to take her to London. 

Margaret received a letter from Mr Bell.

I'm sorry to leave you. I had to return to Oxford on urgent business.

I want you to know that when I die, and I hope it won't be soon, you will inherit[1] everything I own. I am your godfather and I loved your father for thirty-five years. I stood next to him on his wedding day and I closed his eyes when he died. You can write to me and say 'Margaret Hale is not a girl to say no,' or you can write 'No, thanks.'

Margaret wrote to Mr Bell and said 'Margaret Hale is not a girl to say no.' She couldn't think of any other words.

---

1. inherit : money and property received when someone dies.

Margaret went to the Higgins to say goodbye. Nicholas was not there and Mary cried when she heard that Margaret was leaving Milton.

'I would like something to remind me of Bessy,' Margaret said.

Mary gave her a little drinking cup. Next they went to the Thornton's. Mrs Thornton was softer to Margaret now she knew she was leaving. Margaret apologised for her manner[2] the last

---

2. manner : behaviour.

time they had seen each other, but said that she could not give an explanation.

'Miss Hale has called to say goodbye,' Mrs Thornton said to John.

'You're leaving then?' John said.

'Yes,' said Margaret. 'We leave tomorrow.'

When John and Margaret stood next to each other on the doorstep, they both thought about the time when Margaret threw her arms around him to protect him.

That evening, Nicholas Higgins came to say goodbye and Margaret gave him her father's Bible.

'Bless you,' said Nicholas.

The house in London was quiet and luxurious, but Helstone and Milton had felt more like home to Margaret. Her life in London had no purpose and she resumed[3] her role of watching and admiring Edith. Margaret's thoughts often returned to Milton and the people there. She looked forward to Dixon's arrival in London.

One day Mr Bell came to visit and he told Margaret how helpful Mr Thornton had been in settling her affairs.[4] Later in the evening Henry Lennox called.

---

3. resumed : continued after a pause.
4. settling her affairs : helping with money and property.

'Thank you for everything you did for Frederick,' Margaret said.

'I'm sorry that one of Frederick's witnesses was not in London when he was there,' said Henry.

'I didn't know Frederick was in London,' said Mr Bell.

'He was with my mother when she died,' said Margaret.

Mr Bell was not impressed with Henry Lennox and he sensed that Margaret did not want to be left alone with him. Mr Bell suggested a visit to Helstone to see the trees in autumn and asked Margaret if she wanted to come with him.

The next day they caught the train to Helstone, but wherever they went people asked how her father was. Margaret tried to speak and tell them about his death, but she found it difficult.

'He died quite suddenly,' Mr Bell told them, 'on a visit to Oxford.'

Margaret and Mr Bell visited the house where Margaret had lived with her parents. It was very different and the new vicar and his wife had changed it inside and outside. Every room in the house was new and the visit was not what Margaret had expected.

'You remember what we said about Frederick last night,' Margaret said to Mr Bell. 'I want to tell you about something I did which was very wrong. I told a lie.'

'Everyone tells lies. You must have had a good reason. Tell me about it,' he said.

'When Frederick came to Milton my mother was very ill. Dixon told me that she had met someone called Leonards who wanted to collect the reward money for Frederick's arrest. I told Frederick it was too dangerous for him to stay in Milton. I wanted him to go to London and speak to Henry Lennox about clearing his name. I went with him to the railway station. Mr Thornton saw me there with Frederick. I smiled but I didn't speak to him. Frederick pulled away when Leonards tried to grab him and Leonards fell. I later heard that he died. When a policeman came to our house I said that I wasn't at the station, but Mr Thornton knew I was there. I couldn't tell him the truth because I had to keep Frederick's trip to England a secret. Mr Thornton doesn't respect me anymore and I'm so sad about that. Will you tell him everything, Mr Bell?'

Mr Bell nodded. 'Yes, I think he ought to know.'

THINK!

Margaret receives love and financial support from Mr Bell, her father's friend.

1 Why does Mr Bell want to help Margaret?

2 Do you have a family friend who cares about your family?

3 Margaret cares about the Higgins family. Do you have any particular friends you care about?

The text and beyond • page 108
Values & Feelings • page 126

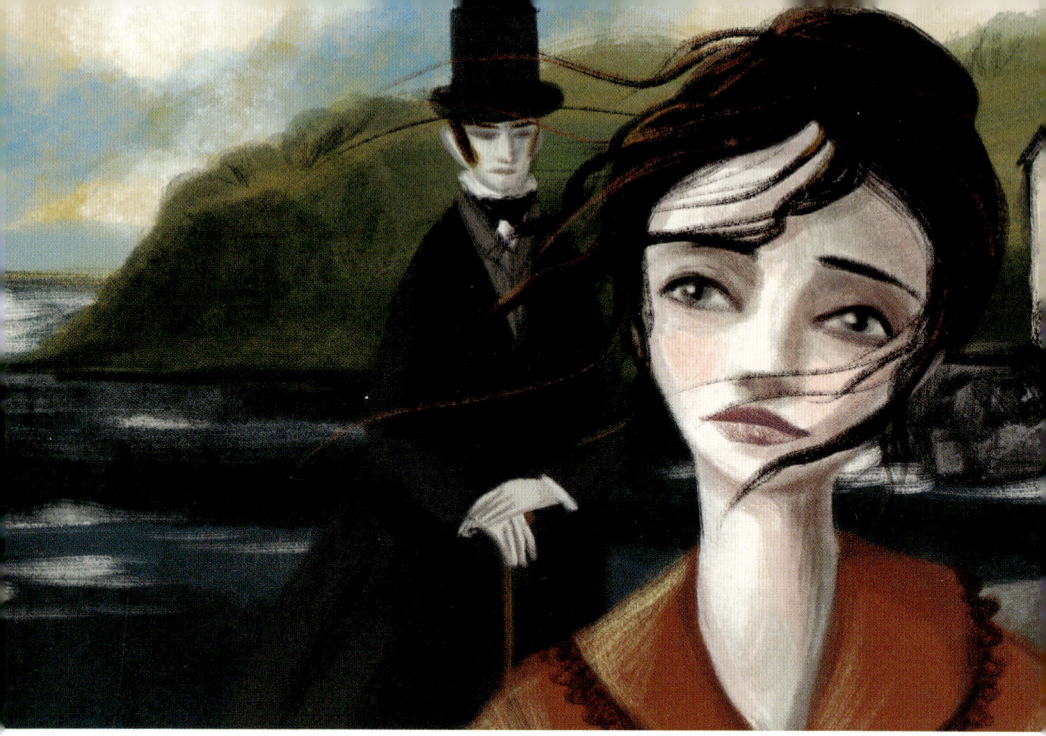

CHAPTER 12

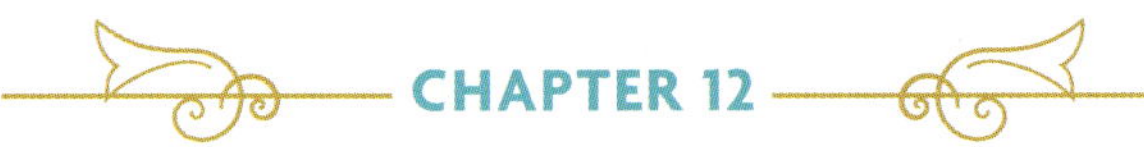

Resolutions

One of Margaret's greatest pleasures at this time was playing with Edith's little boy. He had a strong character but she liked this. She enjoyed spending time with him because she was sure that she would never have children of her own. Margaret was pleased when Dixon arrived bringing all the gossip from Milton. Fanny's wedding had been grand and Mr Thornton had bought some of Margaret's furniture in the sale. Nicholas was well and Mary Higgins was working at Thornton's mill.

track 13

One day Edith said that Mr Bell wanted to take Margaret to visit her brother and sister-in-law in Cádiz. The idea of going to Spain delighted Margaret but Edith was worried that she wouldn't return.

Henry Lennox often came to the house. The two brothers were very different but very close. Edith gave lots of dinner parties and even though Henry and his friends brought wit[1] and knowledge to the evenings, Margaret thought they were superficial and false.

Mr Bell had been unwell, but he planned a visit to see Margaret. On the day of his visit, Mr Bell did not arrive. His servant, a man called Wallis, sent a message saying that the doctor did not expect Mr Bell to survive the night. Edith was shocked and Margaret quickly put on her bonnet.

'I'm going to Oxford. There's a train in half an hour.'

'You can't do that,' said Edith. 'He lives in rooms in college.'

So, Captain Lennox accompanied Margaret. But when they arrived Wallis told them that Mr Bell had died during the night.

When night came Margaret watched the beauty of the London sky. Death taught her what life should be and she prayed to always have the strength to speak and act the truth.

Margaret inherited a large amount of money from Mr Bell and Henry Lennox became her legal advisor. Edith hoped that Margaret and Henry would marry, but Henry was afraid to fail a second time.

There was no trip to Spain that autumn but Margaret did go with the Lennoxes to Cromer, an English seaside town. Margaret sat for hours on the beach, watching the waves. It made her feel better. She thought about her past life and her future and when Henry Lennox arrived he noticed a change in Margaret.

'She looks ten years younger than she did in London,' he said. 'Her eyes are bright, her lips are red and her face is full of peace and light. She is like the Margaret I knew in Helstone.' Henry decided to try very hard and win Margaret's love.

---

1. **wit** : intelligence.

Henry had been to Milton on business and Margaret liked to hear him speak about it. Henry liked the energy of the people, their power and courage.

When they returned from Cromer, Margaret decided to take control of her life and the Lennoxes decided to keep any men away from her. They wanted her only to see Henry.

Business was bad in the town of Milton and John Thornton's business was in trouble. However a strong relationship based on trust had grown between Thornton, Nicholas Higgins and the workers. One day Higgins asked him if he knew anything about Miss Hale.

Thornton smiled. 'Oh, yes. She's my landlord now.'

'Is her brother Mr Frederick alright? He was in Milton when his mother died.'

Finally John Thornton understood that the man he had seen Margaret with at the station was her brother.

John Thornton knew he would have to give up his business and the house and look for a job. Fanny's husband wanted John to take part in some stock market[2] speculation. John's father had been ruined by speculation. It was too risky for John and his workers, so he refused. He also refused to go into partnership[3] with Hamper's son.

It was a hot summer evening when Edith said that Henry had invited John Thornton for dinner. Margaret was surprised.

'Why is John Thornton in London?' she asked.

'His business has failed. He can no longer keep the house and the factory.'

Mr Colthurst, a member of parliament who was interested in Milton, was also present.

---

2. stock market : where stocks and shares are sold.
3. partnership : an arrangement with two people.

John Thornton looked older and tired and he did not look at
Margaret, so she could study him. The dinner was a success and
Mr Colthurst was impressed with Thornton's relationship with his
workers. He believed that friendship brought mutual[4] advantages.
The boss and his workers were unconsciously[5] and consciously[6]
teaching each other.

Suddenly Thornton turned to Margaret and told her that Higgins
and his men had all said that they would like to work for him if he
could employ them again.

As Mr Lennox was leaving Margaret said. 'Can I speak to you
tomorrow? I need your help.'

'Certainly,' Henry's eyes brightened.

'So? Have you asked her to marry you?' Edith asked Henry.

'No, I haven't,' said Henry. 'She won't marry me. She's not interested.'

'Then why did she want to talk to you?' asked Edith.

'Business. I have to bring Mr Thornton with me tomorrow.'

---

4. mutual : for the benefit of two people.
5. unconsciously : without realising one's actions.
6. consciously : realising one's actions.

No one ever knew why Mr Lennox did not come to the meeting the following day. Mr Thornton arrived on time and Margaret was an hour late.

'I want you to take eighteen thousand pounds of my money, which is lying in the bank unused. You can keep the mill going and pay me a better rate of interest.'

John Thornton did not speak. Then he knelt by her side. 'Margaret. If you do not speak I shall understand that you want us to be together.'

'I'm not good enough for you,' said Margaret.

'Look at these,' he said. He took some dried roses from his pocket. 'They are from Helstone. I had to see where you came from. What will Aunt Shaw say when she hears about me. She'll say – That Man!'

Margaret laughed. 'And Mrs Thornton when she hears about me. She'll say – That Woman!'

THINK!

In this chapter, Henry Lennox is hopeful that Margaret will marry him. John Thornton is hopeful that his workers will work for him again.

1 What are your hopes and dreams?
2 Mr Bell's money has given Margaret independence. What do you think are Margaret's hopes and dreams?

The text and beyond • page 110
Values & Feelings • page 126

A novel of contrasts

The main and overriding[1] contrast in the novel is the one between northern and southern Britain. At the height of the Industrial Revolution, the north became the workshop[2] of the country, while London remained the financial and trading centre. The richer south was suddenly poorer, while the north had become rich and influential. In Mrs Gaskell's novel, Margaret Hale represents the refined but penniless south and John Thornton represents the tough, hard-working, self-made man from the north. The situation changed in the 1920s when competition from other countries meant that northern manufacturing declined, resulting in terrible unemployment in the 1930s. The British economy revived but the 'new industries' were mostly based in the south. The contrast between north and south exists even today.

The contrast in setting in the novel is seen through the eyes of the characters. The Hales's sitting room is contrasted with the Thornton's drawing room. It is John who admires the simplicity and comfort of the room. He compares it to his own expensively furnished sitting room which has a cold feel as if it's rarely used.

Comparisons are made between city life and life in the countryside. Margaret contrasts the happiness she feels when she is in the forest

---

1. **overriding :** essential.
2. **workshop :** like a factory where things are made.

near Helstone, with Milton – its factories and the air that smells and tastes of smoke.

Mrs Gaskell makes contrasts in her characters. Margaret compares John Thornton with her father. Mr Hale has a face of almost feminine beauty while John's face is strong and serious and has a rare smile that Margaret particularly likes.

At the heart of the novel is the contrast between industrial growth and efficiency in the mill, versus humanitarianism. Margaret has little interest in industry and money, but she cares about people – poor Bessy Higgins who is dangerously ill from working in the cotton mill.

---

1 Complete the second sentence so that it has a similar meaning to the first sentence, using the word given. You can use between two and three words including the word given.

1. The richer south had suddenly become poorer. (*rich*)
   The south was not .... the north.

2. Many southerners felt superior to people in the north. (*down*)
   Many southerners .... people from the north.

3. Northern manufacturing declined in the 1920s. (*worse*)
   Northern manufacturing .... the 1920s.

4. John thought his sitting room lacked comfort. (*comfortable*)
   John thought his sitting room was .... than Margaret's.

A Condition-of-England novel

Mrs Gaskell wrote during the 'Hungry Forties', a time of acute economic depression and social unrest.

Her contemporary writers, Charles Dickens (*Hard Times*, 1854) and Charlotte Brontë (*Shirley*, 1849), were extremely critical of the era they lived in. *Hard Times* was a radical criticism of an age of economic inequality where the rich were extremely rich and the poor lived in squalor.[1] Industrial workers were underpaid and Mrs Gaskell, Dickens and many other writers expressed their anger towards the increasing system of industrialisation in England.

North and South is often described as a 'Condition-of-England' novel because it uses strong realism and detailed descriptions of inequality and poverty, to highlight social problems and the growing animosity[2] between rich and poor. This type of novel combines story and protest, showing the reader the realities of the working class in 19th century society. It uses exaggeration[3] because hidden around the story is a discussion about the state of England in the early 19th century and a demand for reform.

A Condition-of-England novel documents the suffering of the poor, uses dialect to reflect working-class speech and criticises the effects of industrialisation. At the heart of the novels was a protagonist who has difficult romantic attachments and wants to help the

1. **squalor :** dirty and unpleasant living conditions.
2. **animosity :** dislike/bad feeling.
3. **exaggeration :** to make something seem more.

▶ Patrick Branwell Brontë, *The Brontë Sisters*, circa 1834, National Portrait Gallery, London.

working classes and take on a role as their spokesperson. Both Mrs Gaskell and Charles Dickens' message was heard. Towards the end of the 19th century, legislation brought reform and life did improve for many.

1 Comprehension check • Write brief answers to the questions below.

1. Why was this period called the 'Hungry Forties'?
2. In what way did *Hard Times* criticise this era?
3. Why is *North and South* described as a Condition-of-England novel?
4. What does this type of novel combine?
5. What form does a Condition-of-England novel take?
6. Why is Margaret a typical protagonist for this type of novel?
7. What happened at the end of the 19th century?

The famous kiss

For many fans of period drama,[1] the BBC four-part adaptation of Mrs Gaskell's *North and South* (2004) is still considered to be the best drama of all time. This is strange considering the lack of promotion the BBC gave this series and the lack of expectations.

The series was directed by Brian Percival (the director of *Downton Abbey*) and the novel was adapted by scriptwriter Sandy Welch, known for her screenplays for *Jane Eyre* (2006) and *Emma* (2009). The series is visually stunning because of the beautiful costumes. It is set in the grey and dull landscape of the industrial north, yet one of the most striking[2] scenes is when John Thornton walks through the mill, cotton blowing around him like snow.

The story explores the simmering[3] passion between two people, Margaret Hale and John Thornton, from very different backgrounds, surrounded by the conflict and concerns of social justice and individual responsibility. Lots of questions arise over the course of the four episodes. Are Margaret's ideas about social reform right, or is she interfering in the ways of the north? Does John Thornton care about his workers?

Daniella Denby-Ashe played the refined and socially liberal Margaret. Richard Armitage played the hero John Thornton. The chemistry between the two main characters brought on-screen magic. Viewers had to wait until the end of the fourth episode for the kiss between John and Margaret. British viewers loved it. So many people rushed to leave a message on the BBC's online message board that the system crashed.

---

1. **period drama :** historical drama.
2. **striking :** visually dramatic.
3. **simmering :** slowly bubbling and growing more intense.

1 Look at the stills and answer the questions.

1. Look at still A.
   a Where is this scene set?
   b Who can you see in the still?
   c What could both characters be thinking?

2. Look at still B.
   a What is John Thornton holding in his right hand?
   b Where is he going? Why?

3. Look at still C.
   a Where is Margaret?
   b Why has she gone there?
   c What are the people doing?

An age of steam and smoke

The Industrial Revolution

In the 18th and early 19th century Britain was a rural nation with eighty per cent of the population living in the countryside. Industry in the 18th century was unsophisticated and Britain's economy revolved mostly around agriculture and the textile industry. People worked in their own homes (cottage industries), spinning[1] and weaving,[2] but at the end of the 18th century, a period of great technological invention brought change. The first machines were water driven, but James Watt improved steam engine technology and this meant that coalmines and textile mills could use steam-powered engines. James Hargreaves's 'Spinning Jenny' (a spinning

---

1. **spinning** : making wool from the sheep into thread, by using a machine.
2. **weaving** : making a piece of cloth from thread.

machine with eight wooden spindles) revolutionised cotton spinning in the textile industry. It meant that cheap and light cloth could be mass-produced.

Large factories grew and, as a result of this, transport improved. New roads and a canal system were built and it was quicker and easier to move heavy goods such as coal and iron on canals. It was an age of steam-powered machinery and by the middle of the 19th century fifty per cent of the population lived in overcrowded and unclean cities.

The Corn Laws, which kept the price of corn very high, meant that people were starving and had to look for work in London and the north. People were needed to operate machinery and factories employed many women and children because they could pay them a lower wage. Children could crawl[3] between the machines and repair them. People worked twelve-hour days and there were accidents.

Manchester at the beginning of the 18th century was a small town with a population of less than 10,000, but by the end of the century it had grown to 89,000.

Technological progress brought social unrest. The air and water in these industrial towns was polluted. Rubbish was thrown out of windows onto the streets and the air was filled with black smoke from the factories. Because there was

---

3. crawl : move forward on hands and knees.

now competition amongst the manufacturers, high production costs decreased the manufacturers profits, so they cut wages and people hardly had enough money to live on.

Cities were overcrowded, often ten or twelve people had to share a room in a lodging house, without water or a flushing toilet. People lived, worked and died in very poor conditions and from disease like cholera, typhus and dysentery.

Child labour was the worst problem. In 1833 the government passed a Factory Act to improve conditions for children working in factories.

The hours children could work was strictly regulated and inspectors checked that the law was enforced.

1 Comprehension check • Complete the sentences about the Industrial Revolution.

canals   factories   agriculture   towns   roads   steam

1. The country changed from mostly .... to industry.

2. Cottage industry in homes moved to ....

3. Water and wind power changed to ....

4. There was a revolution in transport with an improvement in .... and ....

5. The population in .... grew.

2 Speaking • Talk to your partner and answer these questions. Then compare your answers with the rest of the class.

1. Do you think it is good to have technological advancement? Why is it good? Is there anything negative about it?

2. What was life like for poor children in industrial towns?

Activities

1 Comprehension check • **Read the first part of each sentence (1-10) and match it with a conclusion (a-l). There are two conclusions that you do not need to use.**

1. ☐ Margaret can see the good in Edith
2. ☐ Captain Lennox and Edith
3. ☐ Margaret has lived in London
4. ☐ Aunt Shaw is wealthy
5. ☐ Margaret's brother Frederick
6. ☐ Margaret loves the countryside in Helstone
7. ☐ Mr Hale seems troubled
8. ☐ Henry Lennox visits Helstone
9. ☐ Mr Hale is leaving the church
10. ☐ Mr Hale wants Margaret

a and tells Margaret he loves her.

b but did not marry for love.

c now she is getting married.

d because he wants to work in industry.

e are moving to Corfu.

f and spends evenings in his study.

g and Margaret promises to marry him.

h to tell her mother they are moving to the north.

i and hates the industrial north.

j for almost ten years.

k because he is having doubts.

l is still away at sea.

Past perfect tense

'Margaret *spoke* gently to her cousin, but she *had fallen* asleep on the sofa.'

We use the past perfect to speak about an action in the past that happened before another past action. We use the past perfect to emphasise which action happened earlier: *had/hadn't* + past participle.

We often use the past perfect tense with *when, after, for, since, already, yet, by the time.*

*Margaret's father was a poor vicar and her parents **had sent** her to London to enjoy life in the city.*

We use *not* for the negative form.

*Despite the fact that Aunt Shaw **had not married** for love, Mrs Hale was jealous of her sister's wealth.*

2 Grammar • Combine the two phrases to make one. Use the word in brackets and the past perfect. There is an example (0).

0. Margaret got ready. She went downstairs to meet the neighbours. (*when*)
When Margaret had got ready, she went downstairs to meet the neighbours.

1. Margaret looked at the shawls. She chose a red one. (*after*)

2. Captain Lennox left. Margaret felt relieved. (*when*)

3. Margaret's father seemed troubled. She thought there was more bad news. (*because*)

4. Henry Lennox drew a picture of Margaret. She felt uncomfortable. (*after*)

3 Vocabulary: feelings • Complete the table with the words in the box.

dizzy   calm   cowardly   uncomfortable   depressed

1	lacking in courage	....
2	losing your balance	....
3	discomfort	....
4	not showing strong emotion	....
5	melancholy/sad	....

1 Comprehension check • **For each question choose the correct answer – a, b, c or d**

1. Who tells Mrs Hale they are leaving Helstone?
   - **a** ☐ Mr Hale
   - **b** ☐ Edith
   - **c** ☐ Margaret
   - **d** ☐ the Bishop

2. Mr Hale is going to become...
   - **a** ☐ bishop
   - **b** ☐ a factory worker
   - **c** ☐ a school teacher
   - **d** ☐ a tutor

3. Milton is...
   - **a** ☐ grey and smoky
   - **b** ☐ restful
   - **c** ☐ a seaside town
   - **d** ☐ sunny

4. Mr Thornton is...
   - **a** ☐ a teacher
   - **b** ☐ a manufacturer
   - **c** ☐ the landlord
   - **d** ☐ a priest

5. Margaret feels more settled in Milton when...
   - **a** ☐ she has Bessy to care about.
   - **b** ☐ she meets Mr Thornton.
   - **c** ☐ she hears from Frederick.
   - **d** ☐ her mother is happier.

2 Vocabulary • **Complete these sentences with adjectives from the text.**

1. Mrs Hale was surprised that her husband wanted to live where the air was

   ....

2. Mr Hale looked grey and ....

3. The house at Helstone had an .... sound.

4. Helstone was a .... place.

5. Margaret was a beautiful and .... woman.

6. Margaret says that John Thornton isn't a .... man.

7. The girls in Milton commented on Margaret's .... clothes.

3 Vocabulary • **Match the words in exercise 2 with their opposite.**

	Word	Opposite
1	....	coarse
2	....	bright
3	....	full
4	....	clean
5	....	plain
6	....	noisy
7	....	modest

4 Writing • **Margaret's mother 'looks forward to a holiday at Heston' by the sea. Write about a holiday or an occasion that you looked forward to and enjoyed.**

- where it was
- who you went with
- was it everything you expected?

....

....

....

....

1 Comprehension check • Answer the questions below.

1. What does Mrs Thornton warn her son about?
2. Why is Mrs Thornton shocked at John's reply?
3. What does John think about the Hale's sitting room?
4. What does John prefer about the north of England in comparison to the south?
5. What did John's mother encourage him to do when he was young?
6. Who does John feel sorry for?
7. Why is John confused by Margaret's southern manners?
8. How does Margaret help Bessy?
9. Do all the Thornton family have strong characters?
10. Why wasn't Mrs Thornton and Fanny's visit a success?

2 Ideas • Match the pieces of text from the story (1-6) with the characters (a-d) and the part of the country they are talking about (north and south). You can use a character more than once. The first has been done for you (0).

0. **b** There is also less suffering.
1. ☐ A working man could climb to the position and power of a boss.
2. ☐ I would rather be working and suffering.
3. ☐ A smokier, dirtier town.
4. ☐ There is less excitement.
5. ☐ Living a dull prosperous life.
6. ☐ The manufacturers were fair with their workers.

a John speaking about the north.
b Margaret speaking about the south.
c John speaking about the south.
d Mrs Hale speaking about the north.

3 Vocabulary • **Find the synonyms in the text for these adjectives.**

	Word	Synonym
1	honest	....
2	solemn	....
3	respected	....
4	well-mannered	....
5	fragile	....

4 Vocabulary • **Complete the sentences with the adjectives in exercise 3.**

1. Mrs Thornton was a severe, ... woman.

2. John Thornton thought that Margaret was .... to him.

3. Margaret liked John's straight eyebrows and .... eyes.

4. The manufacturers in Milton were .... to their workers.

5. John felt sorry for people of .... character.

5 Speaking • **The picture at the beginning of the chapter (on page 20) shows the smoky Milton air.**

1. Even today air pollution is putting people at risk. What can we do about it?

2. How could car sharing help?

3. Should there be more cycle lanes? How could this help?

1 Comprehension check • Are the following sentences true (T) or false (F)? Correct the false ones.

1.	Margaret describes Helstone to Bessy.	**T**	**F**
2.	Bessy is ill because of the cotton dust.	**T**	**F**
3.	Bessy's father didn't know about the white dust.	**T**	**F**
4.	Margaret is worried about her father's ill health.	**T**	**F**
5.	Margaret's brother Frederick was involved in a mutiny.	**T**	**F**
6.	Frederick was court martialled.	**T**	**F**
7.	Frederick is now in Spain and has changed his name.	**T**	**F**
8.	John says that business is as good as last year.	**T**	**F**
9.	If John lowers the wages the workers won't strike.	**T**	**F**
10.	Margaret thinks John is too proud to shake her hand.	**T**	**F**
11.	Mrs Hale thinks she will never see Helstone or Frederick.	**T**	**F**
12.	Mr Hale speaks to the doctor.	**T**	**F**

2 Vocabulary • Read the text below and compete with words from the pool. There is an example at the beginning (0).

> wages   loud   damp   dust   smoke   lungs   cruel   health   ~~hard~~

Life was (**0**) ......*hard*...... for workers in Victorian factories. In the cotton mills (**1**) .... from the cotton got into their (**2**) .... The machines were very (**3**) .... and the noise continued all day. The working day was twelve hours and Sunday was the only day off.

Factory owners paid children low (**4**) .... Children as young as six years old carried out dangerous tasks and were beaten by (**5**) .... masters if they made a mistake. Many workers lived in poor quality housing near the factory. The air was full of (**6**) .... People's (**7**) .... was bad because of the warm, (**8**) .... conditions in the mills. Disease spread and many children died.

3 Vocabulary • Complete the sentences with the words from exercise 2.

1. Bessy is ill because the cotton in the factory creates a white
   .... and it is in her ....

2. Margaret was worried about her mother's ill ....

3. The sailors rose up in mutiny because the Captain was ....
   and unfair.

4. John Thornton may have to reduce the workers' ....

5. The sound from the machines in the mill was very ....
   and conditions inside were warm and ....

6. The Thornton's house was blackened by ....

4 Speaking • Talk to a partner and answer these questions. Then compare your answers with the class.

1. Why do you think people moved to towns to work in terrible conditions
   in factories?

2. Do you think that a twelve hour working day is acceptable?
   Why?/Why not?

3. The workers only had free time on Sunday. What do you think they did
   in their free time?

4. What do you do in your free time?

5 Characters • Who says? Match the character to what they say.

Frederick   John   Bessy   Dr Donaldson   Margaret   Mr Hale

1. .... thinks the air is killing his wife.

2. .... says that the workers are like children.

3. .... tells Margaret her mother is very unwell.

4. .... can never come home to Britain.

5. .... would like to breathe clean air.

6. .... respects and admires John.

1 Comprehension check • Put the sentences (a-l) in the correct order (1-12) to make a summary of Chapter 5.

a ☐ Margaret tells Bessy her mother is dying and her brother is falsely accused of a crime.

b ☐ Mr Hale believes that the men must return to work because their families are starving.

c ☐ The mill workers are on strike because they won't accept lower wages.

d ☐ Nicholas Higgins calls Margaret a southern foreigner who doesn't understand the north.

e ☐ John Thornton's friends ask who the beautiful woman is.

f ☐ Bessy's father Nicholas is on strike.

g ☐ Margaret says that agricultural workers in the south can't strike.

h ☐ Mrs Hale packs a basket of food for the Boucher family who are starving.

i ☐ Margaret explains that the Hales are accepted into society because they are educated.

j ☐ Mr Hale and Margaret are invited to dinner at the Thornton's.

k ☐ Bessy thinks Margaret doesn't have any worries.

l ☐ Margaret looks beautiful at the Thornton's dinner party.

2 Sentence transformation • For each phrase complete the second sentence so that it means the same as the first. Use no more than three words. There is an example at the beginning (0).

0. 'I don't like this strike,' Nicholas said.
Nicholas said he .... *didn't like* .... this strike.

1. Mrs Hale was too weak and unwell to go to the party.
Mrs Hale wasn't .... to go to the party.

2. 'Remember who gave you life.'
'Don't .... who gave you life.'

3. Margaret can't play the piano.
Margaret is .... play the piano.

4. They dine with visitors from parliament.
Visitors from parliament .... with them.

5. Margaret didn't speak and returned home.

Margaret said .... and returned home.

6. Fanny was not as strong as John and his mother.

Fanny was .... than John and his mother.

7. It was the first time their hands had met.

Their hands .... before.

8. Her dignified manner appealed to him.

He .... manner.

9. 'Who is the beautiful and educated woman?' asked his friends.

His friends asked .... and elegant woman was.

Second conditional

If the farm workers *stopped* work there *would be* no seed sown and nothing *would grow*.

We use the second conditional for **unlikely situations** in the present or future.

If + subject + simple past, subject + *would* + verb

If he **had** a lot of money, he **would go** to Australia.

3 Grammar • **Change these sentences into second conditional sentences as in the example.**

0. I don't know the answer. I can't help you.

If I knew the answer I would help you.

1. John finds some money. He takes it to the police.

....

2. Sarah meets a famous person. She asks them some questions.

....

3. I am a rock star. I live in Los Angeles.

....

4. They have a dog. They take it for a walk everyday.

....

1 Comprehension check • **For each question choose the correct answer – a, b, c or d.**

1. When Dixon opens the door...
   - **a** ☐ mrs Hale has died.
   - **b** ☐ mrs Hale is better.
   - **c** ☐ dr Donaldson is with Mrs Hale.
   - **d** ☐ Frederick is with Mrs Hale.

2. When Margaret goes to the Thorntons...
   - **a** ☐ the mill is silent and the atmosphere is angry.
   - **b** ☐ the machines are making a lot of noise.
   - **c** ☐ there is a light, happy mood.
   - **d** ☐ there is no one there.

3. The crowd is angry and Margaret...
   - **a** ☐ takes her wooden shoes off.
   - **b** ☐ throws a stone at the crowd.
   - **c** ☐ protects John Thornton with her arms.
   - **d** ☐ calls for Mrs Thornton.

4. Fanny thinks...
   - **a** ☐ Margaret wants to take charge of the mill.
   - **b** ☐ John doesn't love Margaret.
   - **c** ☐ mrs Hale wants Margaret to marry John.
   - **d** ☐ Margaret wants to marry John.

5. John's tears...
   - **a** ☐ delight Margaret.
   - **b** ☐ make Margaret happy.
   - **c** ☐ entertain Margaret.
   - **d** ☐ make Margaret feel sad.

2 Characters • **There are lots of characters (a-h) in the story who are worried about something (1-8). Match the character to their worry.**

a	Nicholas	**e**	Mr Boucher
b	Mr Hale	**f**	Margaret
c	Mrs Hale	**g**	Frederick
d	John Thornton	**h**	Bessy

1. ☐ does not have enough food for the family.
2. ☐ is concerned about the mill strike.
3. ☐ is upset about the riot.
4. ☐ wants to see Frederick again.
5. ☐ is concerned about Frederick's safety if he comes home.
6. ☐ embarrassed about impulsive behaviour.
7. ☐ concerned about not seeing Margaret again.
8. ☐ worried about capture and court martial.

3 Vocabulary • **Read the definitions and find the correct word for each one using the spaces provided.**

1. To take something for a short period and return it   b _ _ _ _ _
2. A large number of people gathered   c _ _ _ _
3. The tone or mood of a place   a _ _ _ _ _ _ _ _ _
4. When someone has lost consciousness   f _ _ _ _ _ _
5. A person who lacks courage.   c _ _ _ _ _

4 Vocabulary • **Complete the sentences with the words from exercise 3.**

1. John went out of the house to speak to the ....
2. The .... was dark and angry.
3. Margaret goes to the Thornton's house to .... a waterbed.
4. A boy calls John a ....
5. The stone hit Margaret on the head and she ....

1 Comprehension check • Answer the following questions.

1. Why does John Thornton feel foolish?
2. What does Mrs Thornton say about a mother's love?
3. What can John Thornton do for Mrs Hale?
4. Dixon doesn't want to tell Margaret something. What?
5. What is Dixon looking for in Margaret's bedroom?
6. Why does Margaret take Nicholas home with her?
7. Why doesn't Nicholas want to talk to John Thornton?
8. Why does Margaret say that the unions are worse than the bosses?

2 Sequencing the story • Which of the two events a-k do not happen in Chapter 7? Write the other letters in the correct time sequence in the boxes below. The first is done for you.

a Nicholas goes home with Margaret.

b Margaret and her mother are sure their letter to Frederick will arrive soon.

c Mrs Hale has several years to live.

d John rides into the country.

e Margaret says that the unions are worse than the bosses.

f A letter arrives from Edith.

g John takes pears to Mrs Hale.

h Bessy will be buried in Margaret's nightdress.

i Edith invites Margaret and her mother to Corfu.

j Mr Hale asks Nicholas to speak to John Thornton.

k Bessy looks peaceful in death.

1	2	3	4	5	6	7	8	9
d								

3 Vocabulary • **Read the definitions and find the correct word for each one using the spaces provided.**

1. A person who causes trouble   t _ _ _ _ _ _ _ _ _ _ _
2. Inflict a penalty on someone   p _ _ _ _ _
3. A noisy, violent person who disturbs   r _ _ _ _ _
4. Follow the commands of someone   o _ _ _
5. Find an answer to   s _ _ _ _
6. Anxiety   w _ _ _ _ _ _

4 Reading pictures • **Answer the following questions.**

1. Look at the picture on page 46.
   a What are they doing?
   b How do you think they feel?
   c What is Mr Hale saying to Nicholas?

5 Reading • **Match the notes with the person who wrote them.**

1. John   3. Mrs Thornton
2. Edith   4. Hamper

A ....
I know you are in love with 'that girl,' but you must forget her.

B ....
I hope Mrs Hale enjoys the pears. Dr Donaldson told me that she likes them.

C ....
You've caused a lot of trouble amongst the workers. I'm sorry, I can't give you a job.

D ....
The weather is lovely and warm. Bring your mother for a holiday.

1 Comprehension check • Put the sentences below (a-o) into the correct order. The first has been done for you.

a ☐ Margaret goes with Frederick to the station.

b ☐ Frederick gets on the train.

c ☐ Frederick arrives home.

d ☐ Mr Hale tells Frederick to leave.

e ☐ John wonders who Margaret was with at the station.

f **1** Mrs Thornton promises to be a friend to Margaret when her mother dies.

g ☐ Margaret denies being at the station.

h ☐ Frederick pulls away and the man falls off the platform.

i ☐ Mrs Hale dies.

j ☐ A police inspector tells Margaret that a man died because of a fall.

k ☐ An aggressive looking man grabs Frederick.

l ☐ Margaret wants Frederick to speak to the lawyer Henry Lennox.

m ☐ John Thornton sees Margaret with a man.

n ☐ Leonards wants the reward for the capture of Frederick.

o ☐ Margaret accompanies her father to the funeral.

2 Vocabulary • Fill in the missing words from a paragraph about court martial.

> reward   court martial   mutiny   capture   hang   lawyer   charges   clear

In 1661 the first parliament under the newly restored King Charles II passed 'the Naval Discipline Act'.

It introduced the (**1**) ...., a military court, for a wide range of (**2**) .... from (**3**) .... to murder. The navy offered a (**4**) .... for the safe (**5**) .... of an officer.

The officer could employ a (**6**) .... to (**7**) .... their name, but if they were found guilty they were sentenced to (**8**) ....

3 Vocabulary • **Complete the sentences with some of the words in exercise 2.**

1. Master Frederick will .... for .... if they catch him.

2. Frederick wants to talk to a .... and try to fight the .... against him.

3. Frederick hopes to .... his name.

4. Frederick doesn't want the navy to .... him, because he wants to return to the woman he loves.

4 Writing • **Imagine you are the police inspector who visits Margaret. Describe:**
- **your first impression of Margaret –** *proud, intelligent, distant, controlled*;
- **your confusion about the eye witness account;**
- **your suspicions about Margaret.**

Write 150 words.

5 Speaking • **Discuss using the questions to help you.**

1. Mrs Thornton has never believed that Mrs Hale was unwell. How do you feel about John's mother?

2. Has something happened in Mrs Thornton's past to make her seem so hard-hearted?

3. Why can't Mrs Thornton call Margaret by her first name?

4. What are your impressions of Frederick?

6 Prediction • **What happens next? Choose one of the possible answers and give reasons for your choice.**

1. The police officer will return and arrest Margaret.

2. John Thornton will save Margaret from police suspicion.

3. The police officer will question the eye witness again.

I think .... because ......

1 Comprehension check • **Read the first part of each sentence (1-10) and match it with a conclusion (a-l). There are two conclusions that you do not need to use.**

1. ☐ When Margaret wakes
2. ☐ John Thornton is the magistrate
3. ☐ John writes a note to the inspector
4. ☐ An inquest is not necessary
5. ☐ Frederick discussed the court martial with Henry Lennox
6. ☐ John Boucher is found dead
7. ☐ Nicholas wants to help Boucher's widow
8. ☐ John Thornton thinks about the fond look
9. ☐ Mrs Thornton asks Margaret about the young man
10. ☐ Nicholas Higgins waits five hours

a   but Margaret can give no explanation.

b   to tell him of Margaret's guilt.

c   to save Margaret from shame.

d   so he decides to ask Thornton for work.

e   she remembers the lie she told the police inspector.

f   and is now in Spain.

g   at home.

h   Margaret gave the young man at the station.

i   to speak to Thornton.

j   because the medical evidence is insufficient.

k   who saw Leonards die.

l   and Margaret has to tell his wife.

2 Characters • **Match the characters (a-e) with their feelings (1-5) in this chapter.**

- **a** Margaret
- **b** John Thornton
- **c** Police Inspector
- **d** Nicholas
- **e** Betsy

1. ☐ proud
2. ☐ jealous, irritable
3. ☐ sad
4. ☐ ashamed
5. ☐ pleased

3 Vocabulary • **Complete the sentences with adjectives from exercise 2.**

1. Margaret feels .... because John Thornton knows she is a liar.
2. John Thornton is .... of the young man Margaret was with. He is .... at work.
3. Mr Hale and Margaret realize that Nicholas is a .... man.
4. Betsy is .... about her lover Leonards death.
5. The police inspector is .... that there won't be an inquest.

4 Speaking • **Women in the 19th century could not go out with strange men. Margaret risks damaging her reputation by keeping Frederick's visit a secret.**

1. Why does she keep Frederick's secret?
2. How does John feel about the dark, thin, elegant stranger who was with Margaret at the station?
3. Do you find it difficult to keep a secret? Why?/Why not?

1 Comprehension check • Read the passage below and choose the best word for each space. There is an example at the beginning (0).

March brought news of Frederick's marriage to Dolores and there (**0**) .... *a* .... letters from Henry Lennox. He didn't think that Frederick (**1**) .... defend himself at a court martial. Frederick's letters were angry. He said he wouldn't live in England if he (**2**) .... permission to return. This made Margaret cry. She was so fond (**3**) .... Frederick and she felt that all her plans had (**4**) ....

Mr Hale was not well that spring. Margaret was happy when he (**5**) .... to accept an invitation to (**6**) .... with Mr Bell in Oxford. Margaret could do (**7**) .... she wanted. She chatted to their maid Martha about Fanny Thornton's marriage to a rich older gentleman. She read Henry Lennox's letters about Frederick and she thought (**8**) .... John Thornton.

Mr Hale was enjoying his visit to Oxford, but he felt very tired.

'I'm fifty-five years old,' he said to Mr Bell.

'That's young. I'm over sixty,' said Mr Bell.

'If I die, what will happen to Margaret?"

'I will always take care (**9**) .... Margaret,' said Mr Bell.

The next morning when the servant went (**10**) .... Mr Hale's room to wake him, he did not answer. Mr Hale had died during the night.

0. (**a**) were	**b** was	**c** weren't	**d** wasn't
1. **a** can	**b** can't	**c** could	**d** couldn't
2. **a** has	**b** hadn't	**c** hasn't	**d** had
3. **a** in	**b** to	**c** of	**d** towards
4. **a** concluded	**b** failed	**c** ended	**d** finished
5. **a** said	**b** decided	**c** want	**d** concluded
6. **a** stay	**b** rest	**c** share	**d** go
7. **a** which	**b** that	**c** when	**d** what
8. **a** on	**b** over	**c** to	**d** about
9. **a** to	**b** on	**c** of	**d** a
10. **a** out of	**b** into	**c** through	**d** past

2 Comprehension check • **The statements about the story 1-6 are not correct.
Correct them. There is an example.**

0. Margaret told John everything and didn't remain loyal to Frederick.
*Margaret wanted to explain everything to John but she had to remain
loyal to Frederick.*

1. Aunt Shaw and Edith would never return to England.

2. Mr Bell could see that John Thornton and Margaret hated each other.

3. Mr Bell ignores John Thornton when he sees him on the train.

4. Margaret cries when she hears about her father's sudden death.

5. John Thornton is happy that Margaret is going to live in London.

6. Mr Bell tells John that Margaret's brother Frederick was in Milton when
Mrs Hale died.

3 Speaking • **Discuss with a partner and answer the questions below.**

1. Margaret's feelings for John Thornton seem confused. Do you think she
loves him? Why/Why not?

2. Do you think Margaret will marry Henry Lennox? Why/Why not?

3. Four people have died. Do you think anyone else could die?

4 Characters • **Match the character to what has happened in this chapter.**

Edith   Mr Hale   Margaret   Frederick   Nicholas Higgins   Mr Bell

1. .... is given a job at Thornton's Mill.

2. .... notices that John and Margaret are in love.

3. .... sends angry letters.

4. .... dies during his stay in Oxford.

5. .... is going to have another baby.

6. .... feels broken.

1 Comprehension check • Answer the questions below.

1. Why doesn't Aunt Shaw like Milton?

....

2. How will Margaret benefit when Mr Bell dies?

....

3. What does Mary give Margaret? Why?

....

4. Why is Mrs Thornton kinder to Margaret?

....

5. Why does Margaret feel that her life in London has no purpose?

....

6. What does Mr Bell sense about Henry Lennox?

....

7. Why is the visit to Helstone difficult?

....

8. What does Margaret confess to Mr Bell?

....

Ought to

Mr Bell nodded. 'Yes, I think he *ought to know*.'

Ought is different to other auxiliary verbs. It is followed by **to** + **infinitive**. It expresses ideas such as **duty**, **necessity** and **moral obligation**. It is not as forceful as *must* but it is stronger than *should*. Like other modal verbs it does not change form for person.

Ought to is more formal than *should*.

The negative is formed by adding *not: ought not to*. The question form of *ought to* is not very common.

2 Grammar • **Change these sentences using *ought to / ought not to*.**

1. Margaret tells a lie. (*ought not to*)

....

2. Margaret smiles at John Thornton but she doesn't speak to him. (*ought to*)

....

3. Frederick pulls away when Leonards tries to grab him. (*ought not to*)

....

4. Margaret tells the policeman that she wasn't at the station. (*ought not to*)

....

5. Margaret doesn't tell John Thornton the truth. (*ought to*)

....

3 Vocabulary • **Complete the second sentence with a word from the text which has a similar meaning to the word in bold.**

1. Mr Bell stood next to him at his **marriage**.
Mr Bell stood next to him on his ....

2. Margaret asks for something of Bessy's to **remember** her.
Margaret asks for something to .... her of Bessy.

3. Margaret apologised for her **behaviour**.
Margaret apologised for her ....

4. She could not give a **reason** for this.
She could not give an .... for this.

5. The house in London was **beautiful** and **expensive**.
The house in London was ....

6. The new **priest** and his wife had changed the house in Helstone.
The new .... and his wife had changed the house in Helstone.

4 Writing • **Write a letter from Margaret to John Thornton. In your letter explain:**
- **why you told the police officer a lie;**
- **what happened at the station;**
- **why you couldn't speak until now about Frederick;**
- **apologise for any dishonesty.**

Write 150 words.

1 Comprehension check • **Read the first part of each sentence (1-10) and match it with a conclusion (a-l). There are two conclusions that you do not need to use.**

1. ☐ Margaret loved her nephew
2. ☐ Mr Bell suggested going with Margaret
3. ☐ Mr Bell had died
4. ☐ A holiday at the seaside
5. ☐ John Thornton learns that the man at the station
6. ☐ John Thornton is in London
7. ☐ John tells Margaret
8. ☐ Henry realises
9. ☐ Margaret used her money
10. ☐ Everyone will be surprised

a   that Higgins and the men want to work for him.

b   to visit Frederick in Cadiz.

c   made Margaret feel much better.

d   to help Henry Lennox.

e   to keep the mill going.

f   because she believed she wouldn't have any children.

g   and left Margaret nothing.

h   was Margaret's brother.

i   when John and Margaret become engaged.

j   that Margaret won't marry him.

k   because his business has failed.

l   and left Margaret a large amount of money.

2 Odd one out • Choose the word that does not belong in each line.

1.	distant	remote	close	detached
2.	tenant	resident	occupant	landlord
3.	risky	safe	secure	protected
4.	nursery	school	college	primary school
5.	wave	beach	sand	sandcastle
6.	boat	ship	cruise ship	train

3 Vocabulary • Now complete the sentences below with the odd words in exercise 2.

1. Mr Bell lives in rooms in .... in Oxford.
2. When Mr Bell is unwell Margaret catches the .... to Oxford.
3. Margaret sits on the beach watching the ....
4. The Lennox brothers are different but very ....
5. It was too .... to speculate because John's father had lost his money on the stock market.
6. Margaret became John's ....

4 Word search • Find the odd words in the word square.

T	R	A	I	N	T	E	W	A	V	E	E	R
C	L	O	S	E	E	T	E	S	N	E	M	R
A	S	R	S	A	N	D	C	A	S	T	L	E
I	K	C	I	L	A	N	D	L	O	R	D	S
S	Y	U	N	S	N	E	R	E	N	C	C	I
O	A	P	D	A	K	B	E	A	C	H	H	D
U	T	A	B	I	C	Y	C	L	E	E	O	E
C	O	L	L	E	G	E	T	E	L	D	O	N
B	F	T	D	I	S	T	A	N	T	A	L	T

1 The meeting • Listen to Margaret and John talking about the meeting with Nicholas Higgins and the other men. Choose the correct answer to the questions.

track 14

1. What time is the meeting?
   a ☐ 9.30 am
   b ☐ 11.00 am
   c ☐ 1 pm
   d ☐ 2 pm

2. Where will they hold the meeting?
   a ☐ small sitting room
   b ☐ drawing room
   c ☐ Lennox's office
   d ☐ spare office

3. How many people are coming?
   a ☐ 3
   b ☐ 5
   c ☐ 7
   d ☐ 10

4. What can they give them to drink?
   a ☐ water
   b ☐ orange juice
   c ☐ tea
   d ☐ coffee

5. What can they give them to eat?
   a ☐ cake
   b ☐ fruit tart
   c ☐ biscuits
   d ☐ sandwiches

2 The North of England • **Listen to Margaret speaking about living in the north of England. Answer the questions briefly. Base your answers on what Margaret says and not on your own opinions.**

1. How does Margaret feel about her life at Aunt Shaw's when she returns to London?
2. How does she feel about Edith's friends?
3. Where are the people Margaret cares about?
4. What job does Margaret have to do?
5. How is Margaret positive now towards the Industrialists?
6. How does Margaret feel about Milton now?

3 Queen Victoria • **Listen to the speaker speaking about Queen Victoria who became queen at the age of 18.**

1. Victoria was .... in line to the throne.
   a first **b** fourth **c** fifth **d** sixth

2. How long was Queen Victoria's reign?
   a 18 years **b** 80 years **c** 60 years **d** 64 years

3. What was Queen Victoria's first language.
   a English **b** French **c** German **d** Italian

4. What was her favourite hobby?
   a sport **b** painting **c** playing the piano **d** cooking

5. How many grandchildren did Victoria and Albert have?
   a 14 **b** 40 **c** 9 **d** 37

6. Who died suddenly when she was only 42?
   a Victoria **b** Albert **c** Victoria's mother **d** a grandchild

7. Where is Victoria buried?
   a Scotland **b** London **c** The Isle of Wight **d** Windsor

Cottonopolis

At the beginning of the 18th century, Manchester was a small market town with 10,000 inhabitants. By 1852 there were over 400,000 people living there. Manchester was the workshop of the world. There were lots of cotton mills and it became known as Cottonopolis.

Use an Internet search engine to find information about these places and answer the questions.

1. Why did people want to work in the cotton mills?

2. What was the work like in the cotton mills?

3. What kind of power did the cotton mills use?

4. When did the term Cottonopolis come into use?

5. Where did cotton merchants meet?

6. Why was Manchester also called 'the Warehouse City'?

7. Why was the air in the mills kept hot and humid?

8. What did the cotton dust do to the workers?

1 GESE GRADE 7 – Early memories • **In the novel *North and South* Margaret has very happy memories of her early life at Helstone. Now think about your own country or town and answer the following questions.**

    a What is your earliest memory? What games did you use to play when you were very young?

    b Do you have brothers and sisters? Did you use to spend a lot of time with siblings or cousins when you were very young?

    c Do you remember your first summer holiday? Were you excited? Where would your family go? To the seaside or to the mountains? What did you use to do on holiday?

2 GESE GRADE 7 – Village or city life • **Margaret likes living in the small village in Helstone and finds it difficult when they move to a town. Answer the questions below.**

    a If you had the choice, would you live in a village or a city? Why?

    b Is it difficult for teenagers to live in a small village? Why? Why not? How would their lives be different if they lived in a town or city?

    c What could be the benefits of living in a village? Should a family with young children live in a village or in a town? Why?/Why not?

3 GESE GRADE 7 – Pollution and recycling • **Milton is an industrial town and very smoky. Answer the questions below.**

    a Do you think it's important to reduce pollution in our towns and cities? How could this be done?

    b What should we do about traffic in our towns and cities to reduce pollution?

    c What could car manufacturers do to help this problem?

    d What does your family recycle at home? Why is it important to recycle?

    e Is there anything else that you think we should recycle?

1 READING AND USE OF ENGLISH PART 1 • For questions 1-10 read the text below and decide which answer (a, b c or d) best fits each gap.

Margaret's parents had sent her to live with Aunt Shaw in London for ten tears, so Margaret could (**0**) ....*b*.......... city life and become a more (**1**) .... young woman. Margaret had always (**2**) .... that her mother and her aunt were jealous (**3**) .... each other. Margaret's parents were (**4**) .... wealthy nor fashionable and Mrs Hale (**5**) .... her sister's wealth and fine lifestyle. Aunt Shaw was (**6**) .... unsettled (**7**) .... her sister's happy marriage. Aunt Shaw had married for money and social status and not for love, but she was determined that her only daughter, Edith, (**8**) .... not make the same mistake. Edith loved Captain Lennox because he was tall and handsome. She loved him (**9**) .... the fact that he didn't have a beautiful house and (**10**) .... a title.

0.	**a** confirm	**(b)** experience	**c** clarify	**d** deserve
1.	**a** advanced	**b** assisting	**c** co-operating	**d** accomplished
2.	**a** knew	**b** know	**b** knows	**d** known
3.	**a** of	**b** by	**b** with	**d** to
4.	**a** neither	**b** either	**b** nor	**d** or
5.	**a** envious	**b** envy	**b** envied	**d** envies
6.	**a** same	**b** equal	**b** equally	**d** instead
7.	**a** of	**b** by	**b** to	**d** with
8.	**a** ought	**b** oughtn't	**b** have	**d** should
9.	**a** despite	**b** although	**b** however	**d** instead
10.	**a** without	**b** lacked	**b** including	**d** holding

2 WRITING PART 2 (letter) • Imagine you are Margaret. Write a letter to your mother telling her about Edith and Captain Lennox. Tell your mother:

- **what Captain Lennox is like and how happy they are;**
- **how much you have enjoyed these years in London;**
- **how excited you are about returning to Helstone.**

Write your letter in 140-190 words.

3 READING AND USE OF ENGLISH PART 3 • Read the text below. Use the word given in capitals at the end of some of the lines to form a word that fits the gap in the same line. There is an example at the beginning (0).

Victorian Society

One of the things that was (0) .....*vitally*..... important in   **VITAL**
Victorian society was good etiquette.

Victorian women were (1) .... about the   **ADVICE**
(2) .... of jewelry for every occasion.   **CHOOSE**

There were strict rules for almost everything – who to dance
with and how. It was all critical (3) ....   **KNOW**

Women's clothing was (4) .... uncomfortable and   **EXTREME**
most women were only (5) .... when their waists were   **SATISFACTION**
very tiny.

Running a house in the 19th century was (6) .... without   **POSSIBLE**
at least one servant. Servants were a sign of (7) ....   **SOCIETY**
standing and the (8) .... was to show off with more   **TEND**
servants than was (9) .... necessary.   **STRICT**

4 WRITING PART 2 (review) • Write 140-190 words in an appropriate style.

You see this announcement in a film and TV magazine.

Next month is History month and we're interested in hearing about any historical period dramas set during the Industrial Revolution. Can you recommend any? Write a review and send it to us. Explain what it is about. Why you liked it. What you learned about this historical period.

Write your review of *North and South*.

....
....
....
....
....
....
....
....

5 READING AND USE OF ENGLISH PART 4 • Complete the second sentence so that it has a similar meaning to the first sentence, using the word given. Do not change the word given. You must use between two and five words, including the word given. Here is an example.

0. 'Your description is like a picture,' said Henry.
COMPARED
Henry ..... *compared her description* ..... to a picture.

1. There had not been enough money to buy her a new dress.
INSUFFICIENT
There .... to buy her a new dress.

2. Margaret thought they were hiding some bad news.
KEEPING
Margaret thought they were .... from her.

3. Soon, we will all forget Helstone.
REMEMBER
Soon, we .... Helstone.

4. They didn't have anywhere to live in Milton.
NOWHERE
They .... live in Milton.

5. Margaret liked to listen to the sea.
PLEASURE
Margaret's .... listening to the sea.

6. The air tasted of smoke.
SMOKY
The air ....

7. Margaret missed Helstone.
HOMESICK
Margaret .... Helstone.

8. Thornton thought it was wrong for people not to improve their positions.
BELIEVE
Thornton .... people not improving their positions.

9. Mrs Thornton and Fanny didn't want to visit the Hale's again.
NOR
Neither Mrs Thornton .... to visit the Hale's again.

a Margaret   **b** John Thornton   **c** Bessy   **d** Nicholas

Which character

1. talks about the white cotton dust? ....
2. goes to the train station with Frederick? ....
3. doesn't like the strike or the riot? ....
4. says her life is not what it seems? ....
5. would like to breathe clean air? ....
6. says business is not as good as the year before? ....
7. asks about the countryside? ....
8. wants to get workers from Ireland? ....
9. thinks the mills are doing well? ....
10. would like to talk to Thornton about money? ....
11. has a dignified manner and a strong character? ....
12. tells the police Inspector a lie? ....
13. is jealous of the young man at the station? ....
14. is looking after Boucher's widow and children? ....
15. buys pears for Mrs Hale? ....

7 READING AND USE OF ENGLISH PART 7 • **Four people (A-D) have reviewed four books. For each statement (1-10) decide which person and book the statement refers to. The people may be chosen more than once.**

A

Flora: *The English Patient* by Michael Ondaatje

This book tells the story of four damaged lives that become entangled at the end of the Second World War. It is a story about love and the elusive search for identity. Ondaatje does not give the reader a linear story and for people who like a plot driven story, this book is too literary and poetic. The characters all have their problems and at the heart of this book is the burnt and broken English Patient.

B

Tim: *The Hunger Games* by Suzanne Collins

I don't usually read dystopian fiction but I decided to read the books before I saw the films. The heroine is sharp and intelligent and the setting is exotic and unique. It's an exciting story but it's gruesome... possibly too gruesome. The first person narrator means that the reader is very close to the main character, but it also means that the other characters have less depth. I don't think children should read this book.

C

Matthew: *Skellig* by David Almond

Oh, I loved this book. It's classified as a children's book but it can be read by all ages. Michael's life is turned upside down. His baby sister is very unwell and Michael's family has moved into a very old house that needs renovating. He goes into the dusty garage and finds a stranger who is more like a creature – some sort of owl man or angel. He shares this secret with Mina, the girl next door. It's a very moving story and made me cry.

D

Eve: *To Kill a Mocking Bird* by Harper Lee

I suppose I like this book because it's about courage. Atticus Finch needs a lot of courage to defend a black man in southern America in the 1930s. He tells his children Jem and Scout to hold their heads high. There is sadness and happiness in this book, racism and equality, immaturity and maturity.

Which person read a book which...

1. has an unusual setting.   ....
2. is set in the 1940s.   ....
3. is set in the US.   ....
4. has a mystical character with wings.   ....
5. is a novel of contrasts.   ....
6. is classed as literary fiction.   ....
7. has less developed minor characters.   ....
8. has a touching story.   ....
9. is poetic with little plot.   ....
10. is written for teenagers.   ....

8 WRITING PART 2 (article) • Write 140-190 words in an appropriate style. Are you a budding writer? We are looking for articles that could feature in our magazine on family life.

- Are you an only child or do you have a sibling like Margaret Hale?
- What are the advantages and disadvantages of being an only child?
- If you could have another sibling, would you prefer to have a sister or a brother? Why?
- What do you think are the pros and cons of a large family?

....

....

....

....

....

....

....

....

....

....

LET'S REVISE THE STORY

1 PICTURE SUMMARY • Put the pictures from the story in the right order. Write a sentence under each one describing the scene.

a	 b	 c
 d	 e	 f
 g	 h	 i
 j	 k	 l

2 COMPREHENSION CHECK • **Answer the questions below about the chapters.**

1. Why does Margaret's life change at the beginning of the story?
2. What is Mr Hale's problem in the first two chapters? How is it resolved?
3. How does Margaret feel about Henry Lennox when he comes to Helstone?
4. What doesn't she like about Henry?
5. What is John Thornton's first impression of Margaret?
6. What are Mrs Thornton's concerns about Margaret?
7. How does Margaret first meet Bessy? How does this meeting change Margaret's life?
8. Why is the smoky air a concern for Mrs Hale's health?
9. Why does Margaret not confide in John Thornton about the lie?
10. Why is Mr Bell an important character in the story?
11. When does Margaret realise she loves John Thornton?
12. How does Margaret feel about the north at the end of the novel?

3 TEST YOUR MEMORY! • **Say in which place these things happen.**

1. Henry Lennox asks Margaret to marry him. ....
2. It's a restful place and Margaret and her mother breathe sea air.

   ....
3. A riot. ....
4. A man takes Frederick by the collar. ....
5. Nicholas waits for five hours to speak to John Thornton. ....
6. Mr Hale dies suddenly. ....
7. Margaret plays with Edith's little boy. ....
8. Margaret goes on holiday with the Lennoxes. ....
9. Margaret wants to return with John Thornton. ....

4 WHAT HAPPENS WHEN...? • **Read each sentence (1-10) and match it with a conclusion (a-j).**

1. ☐ Edith and Margaret are like sisters
2. ☐ Mr Hale decides to leave the church
3. ☐ Milton is smokier and dirtier
4. ☐ John Thornton likes Margaret
5. ☐ Margaret feels needed
6. ☐ Because of the mutiny on the ship
7. ☐ Mr Hale's friend Mr Bell
8. ☐ Bessy dies
9. ☐ The strike has a bad effect
10. ☐ Margaret lends Thornton money

a   because of the cotton fibres in her lungs.

b   and she returns his love.

c   but thinks she is proud.

d   leaves all his money to Margaret.

e   but everything changes when she marries Captain Lennox.

f   when she has Bessy to look after.

g   and asks Margaret to tell her mother.

h   on the business at the mill.

i   than they had ever imagined.

j   Frederick has to live in Spain.

5 INTERVIEW • **At the end of the story, Margaret owns the mill in Milton. A journalist wants to interview her for the newspaper. Imagine you are interviewing Margaret. Continue the interview with at least five more questions and answers. Begin like this:**

Interviewer: *I am delighted to meet you, Miss Hale. Our readers will be interested to hear about your move to the north of England and about the mill which you now own. How do you like it here in Milton?*

Margaret: *I like the north very much, though it has taken me a little while to adjust. The south is very different.*

Interviewer: *Can you tell our readers about your life in the south?*

6 WHICH CHAPTER? • **Look at the phrases and decide which chapter they come from. There is one phrase for each chapter.**

a   The police inspector says there will be no inquest into the death of Leonards. ....

b   Margaret tells Bessy that her mother is dying and her brother is falsely accused of a crime. ....

c   Margaret inherits a large amount of money from Mr Bell. ....

d   Margaret tells her mother they're going to live in Milton-Northern and her father is leaving the church. ....

e   Bessy's face has the soft smile of eternal rest. ....

f   Margaret, who is nineteen, is going to live in Helstone again. ....

g   Margaret and Mr Bell travel to Helstone and visit Margaret's old house. ....

h   John Thornton tells Margaret that he loves her. ....

i   Mrs Thornton was poor when her husband lost all their money and killed himself. ....

j   Frederick arrives and wants to help his mother. ....

k   Bessy tells Margaret that the dust in her lungs is poisoning her. ....

l   Mr Bell, Mr Hale's old friend from Oxford, comes to visit. ....

 THE CHARACTERS

1 **Use the words in the box to help you describe the characters below using a verb: *show*, *feel*, *be*. For example: *is proud*, *feels sad*, *shows anger*. Some of the adjectives can be used for more than one character.**

insensitive • honest • determined • biased • likes a challenge •
a hero • full of regret • love • self-aware • a gentleman • proud •
fair minded • strong character • kind-hearted • mature •
ambitious • good worker • hasty • quick tempered • bitter •
suspicious • sensitive • weak • sceptical • just • fair

 THINK!

2 **Which values and feelings do you think each chapter is about? Go back to each chapter and find the words that describe how people feel, what people value and what is important to them. Then complete the table below.**

Chapters 1-3 ▶

Chapters 4-6 ▶

Chapters 7-9 ▶

Chapters 10-12 ▶

 ## THE STORY

In the word cloud you can see a list of adjectives expressing feelings: which ones can you associate with *North and South*? Justify your answers and write them in the boxes, dividing them into 'positive' and 'negative'.

weak spirited **dishonest** insensitive poor
easy-going **simple** **proud**
hard-working **strong** polluted
kind-hearted **greedy** **honest** sly
shy fair **scared** **clean** stubborn
spoilt **wealthy** prejudiced
selfish complex **ambitious** **just**

POSITIVE

NEGATIVE

 ## YOUR TURN!

4 **What about you? Which feelings and values do you think matter the most? Now prepare your own word cloud using the words above. Make them big or small according to the importance they have for you.**

This reader uses the expansive reading approach: where reading is not only the enjoyment of the story and the discovery of a new language, but an opportunity to make cultural connections.

The new language introduced in this step of our **Reading & Training Life Skills** series is listed below and language from lower steps is included too. For a complete list for all six steps, see *The Black Cat Graded Readers Handbook* at *blackcat-cideb.com*.

Step FOUR B2.1

Verb tenses

Present Perfect Simple: *the first / second etc. time that ...*
Present Perfect Continuous: unfinished past with *for* or *since* (duration form)

Verb forms and patterns

Passive forms: Present Perfect Simple
Reported speech introduced by precise reporting verbs
(e.g. *suggest, promise, apologise*)

Modal verbs

Be / get used to + -ing: habit formation
Had better: duty and warning

Types of clause

3rd Conditional: *if* + Past Perfect, *would(n't) have*
Conditionals with *may / might*
Non-defining relative clauses with: *which, whose*
Clauses of concession: *even though; in spite of; despite*

Step Four

If you enjoyed this reader, try another one in Step Four...

- *Northanger Abbey*, by Jane Austen
- *The Woman in White*, by Wilkie Collins
- *The Turn of the Screw*, by Henry James

Step Five

...or take a step forward to Step Five!

- *Pride and Prejudice*, by Jane Austen
- *Great Expectations*, by Charles Dickens
- *A Tale of two Cities*, by Charles Dickens